Stop Shrinking Back

A Devotional Memoir

By Dr. Stephanie Chambers

Manufactured in the United States of America

ISBN: 979-8-9917255-5-2
Library of Congress Control Number: 2025902189

Follow Authors name
Email: Email:info@stopshrinkingback.com or stopshrinkingback@gmail.com
Website: stopshrinkingback.com

Table of Contents

Acknowledgments

My greatest strength and inspiration is found in the Word of God. I give the highest praise to my heavenly Father and Creator. Without Him I am nothing. All glory to You, Almighty God.

I am forever indebted to my parents for their hard work and sacrifices, and for their love and support. Thank you. My children are my gifts and they continually encourage me to be a better me. I love you immensely. To my brother, my nephew, and their children, God is with us. The Chambers family, thank you for your unwavering love and support. I appreciate and cherish the loyalty and cohesiveness of our families.

The legacy of my maternal grandmother Elizabeth Forrester and great grandmother, Miriam Hooke endures. I recognize their dedication, strength, and perseverance. May they both continue to rest in peace. The love and fortitude of my paternal grandparents, Alice and Neheimah Chambers, remain with me and reverberates throughout generations. My uncles, aunts, and cousins – I love you. The children and I cherish you. To my remaining family members and friends, thank you for your love.

To my mentors – both professional and spiritual God bless you. I must acknowledge my faith-based community: the Way International (Mr. Eustace and Mrs. Denise Martin, Mr. Chris and Mrs. Angie

Gramilch, Mr. Peter and Mrs. Beth Anderson). The Daniel Fast Family, Vine Church (Mr. Richard and Mrs. Yannique Griffiths), Bronx Bethany (Dr. Cheryl Tugman, Shemekia Samuels, Pastor Joy), and Mr. and Mrs. David Tyree, Ms. Janelle Gumbs. You have been integral to my spiritual journey. Thank you for your hearts that are bent towards service, loving, and ministering. Your patience and obedience are noteworthy. Thank you for sharpening me with the Word and for your presence in my life.

Finally, Dr. Miriam Pinion thank you for cheering me on through some of my darkest days. Mr. and Mrs. Guzman, Ms. Colette Brown, Mr. and Mrs. Barnaby, I am grateful for your love and encouragement. Dr. Denise Nicholson, thank you for encouraging me to share my story and for providing a nurturing community and platform to grow in. And to all my friends and colleagues who are not mentioned – a grand thank you.

Foreword

The evidence of God's love and power are made obvious through our life stories or testimonies. "How can I best showcase my love for You, Lord? How can I help to spread Your word to others while overcoming my own fears, trials and tribulations?" In sharing our stories, we allow for the works of God to be manifested through us for others to see. Sharing my story is how I choose to showcase my love for God, the Father and His Son, Jesus Christ. "This is my story and this is my song: praising my Savior all day long." The words of this song speak to my intention in writing, "Stop Shrinking Back". My story is a song of triumph and victory. It is a never-ending quest to turn my tests into a testimony.

The book begins with an acknowledgement of the glorious and limitless nature of God. The true nature of God cannot be understood fully with our limited minds, but a general understanding can be attained with the list of names and attributes referenced in the Word. To know God's name is to know Him and how He reveals Himself through His names. I share my story in hopes to glorify God the Father and Creator of all things, through acknowledgment of His Son, Jesus Christ. My testimony is unique to me, but we each have a testimony. We each have a testimony deep within us. It is in sharing the stories and these experiences that can bring others closer to the Spiritual Source. My source is God through Christ. The gospels record the birth, life, death, and resurrection of Jesus Christ, which bring the promise of salvation. It is a reminder that, even in times of turmoil and tribulation, we are to keep running, enduring to the end, and finishing the race well, all while keeping our eyes on the prize. Our prize is the salvation that comes with knowing that we are justified by faith. Though the trials of life may cause us to shrink back in our thoughts and actions, we can have peace with God through Jesus Christ and through our faith.

May you be encouraged and may your faith be strengthened as you change the patterns of your thinking and live according to God's will. His Word is His will. May we draw closer to the One God and our Father in faith, as we seek Him and get to know Him by **HIS NAME(S)**.

"Forgive me, Father, when I shrink back or dim the light and the power that resides within me. Allow this glorious Light to shine forth to bring You glory. May this book serve as a testament to my love and my devotion to You. As I earnestly search to find You, I find You seeking me. Touch my mind and heart with Your hands, so I may find the words to authentically honor You and empower others. Help me along this journey, to remain steadfast and resilient in the face of adversity. May we resemble the disciples in their zeal and efforts to spread the gospel despite our chains. I pray my words are acceptable and pleasing to You. May they offer guidance, strength, support, and encouragement to those in need, in Jesus' name I pray, amen."

And those who know Your name will put their trust in You, for You, Lord, have not abandoned those who seek You.
– Psalm 9:10

The Names of GOD

Names carry a powerful significance and reflect a person's character, nature, and destiny. Each name listed below reveals a different aspect of God's character, His ways, who He is, and His works . When you really know God and understand the meaning of the names of God, it will fill your heart with faith and confidence. We can rely on the specific aspect of His power and better identify with Him. In identifying with Him we can experience victory and **stop shrinking back**. We can use the names of God in our efforts to rise above tests and trials.

❖ "**<u>Ehyeh-Asher-Ehyeh:</u>** the Hebrew name, I will be what I will be or I Am who I Am".
   Moses said to God, "Suppose I go to the Israelites and say to them, The God of your fathers has sent me to you, and they ask me, What is his name, Then what shall I tell them?" God said to Moses, "I am who I am. This is what you are to say to the Israelites: I Am has sent me to you. " God also said to Moses: Say to the Israelites, 'The Lord, the God of your fathers – the God of Abraham, the God of Isaac and the God of Jacob – has sent me to you. This is my name forever, the name you shall call me from generation to generation." Exodus 3:13-15 NIV

- ❖ <u>**Elohim:**</u> the Hebrew name for God; Plural for supreme power (s) of God.

  In the beginning, God created the heavens and the earth. Genesis 1:1.

- ❖ <u>**Yahweh**</u>: the Hebrew name for God, meaning I Am, The Self-Existent One. I Am. He was. He is. He always has been and always will be. He is the Self-Existent One with no beginning and no end.

  God replied to Moses, "I am who I am. Say this to the people of Israel: I Am has sent me to you." God also said to Moses, "Say this to the people of Israel: Yahweh,_the God of your ancestors – the God of Abraham, the God of Isaac, and the God of Jacob – has sent me to you. This is my eternal name, my name to remember for all generations. Exodus 3:14-15.

- ❖ <u>**El Roi:**</u> the Hebrew name for God, meaning the God who sees me.

  Thereafter, Hagar used another name to refer to the Lord, who had spoken to her. She said, "You are the God who sees me."_She also said, "Have I truly seen the One who sees me?" So that well was named Beer-lahai-roi (which means "well of the Living One who sees me"). Genesis 16:13-14.

- ❖ <u>**El Shaddai:**</u> the Hebrew name for God, meaning The All-Sufficient One, God Almighty.

When Abram was ninety-nine years old, the Lord appeared to him and said, "I am El-Shaddai – 'God Almighty.' Serve me faithfully and live a blameless life. I will make a covenant with you, by which I will guarantee to give you countless descendants." Genesis 17:1-2. See also Gen 28:3. "May God almighty bless you and make you fruitful and multiply you so that you become an assembly of people." Gen 35:11, " God also said to him, "I am God Almighty. Be fruitful and multiply. A nation, indeed an assembly of nations, will come from you, and kings will descend from you."

❖ **El Olam:** is the Hebrew name for God, meaning He has no beginning and no end. He is the Everlasting God or the Eternal God.

After making their covenant at Beersheba, Abimelech left with Phicol, the commander of his army, and they returned home to the land of the Philistines. Then Abraham planted a tamarisk tree at Beersheba, and there he worshiped the Lord, the Eternal God. Genesis 21:32-33.

❖ **Yahweh-Yireh:** the Hebrew name for God, meaning the Lord will provide.

Then Abraham looked up and saw a ram caught by its horns in a thicket. So he took the ram and sacrificed it as a burnt offering in place of his son. Abraham named the place Yahweh-Yireh (which means "the Lord will provide"). To this day, people still use that name as a proverb: "On the mountain of the Lord it will be provided." Genesis 22:13-14.

❖ **Adonai:** the Hebrew name for God, meaning Lord and Master. It is the generic term for lord in Hebrew. It is first seen in scripture when Abram, longing for an heir, cries out to God. I said to the Lord, "You are my Master! Every good thing I have comes from you." Psalm 16:2.

❖ **Yahweh Rapha:** the Hebrew name for God, meaning the Lord who heals. God is our Healer, in both body and soul!
He said, "If you will listen carefully to the voice of the Lord your God and do what is right in his sight, obeying his commands and keeping all His decrees, then I will not make you suffer any of the diseases I sent on the Egyptians; for I am the Lord who heals you." Exodus 15:26.

❖ **Yahweh Nissi:** the Hebrew name for God, meaning the Lord is my banner. The name Yahweh Nissi only appears once in the Bible in Genesis 17:15.
Moses built an altar there and named it Yahweh-Nissi (which means "the Lord is my banner"). Exodus 17:15.

❖ **Qedosh Yisrael:** the Hebrew name for God, meaning Holy One of Israel.
The Lord also said to Moses, "Give the following instructions to the entire community of Israel. You must be holy because I, the Lord your God, am holy. Leviticus 19:1-2.

❖ **Yahweh Shalom:** the Hebrew name for God, meaning the Lord is peace.

And Gideon built an altar to the Lord there and named it Yahweh-Shalom (which means "the Lord is peace"). The altar remains in Ophrah in the land of the clan of Abiezer to this day. Judges 6:24.

❖ **Yahweh Tsuri**: the Hebrew name for God, meaning the Lord is my rock.

The Lord is my rock, my fortress, and my savior; my God is my rock, in whom I find protection. He is my shield, the power that saves me, and my place of safety. Psalm 18:2.

❖ **Yahweh Roh-i**: the Hebrew name for God, meaning the Lord is my Shepherd.

The Lord is my shepherd; I have all that I need. Psalm 23:1.

❖ **El Elyon**: the Hebrew name for God, meaning God Most High. God is supreme. He deserves all our focus, worship, and praise.

I will thank the Lord because he is just; I will sing praise to the name of the Lord Most High. Psalm 7:17.

❖ **Miqweh Yisrael**: the Hebrew name for God, meaning Hope of Israel.

O Lord, you alone are my hope. I've trusted you, O Lord, from childhood. Psalm 71:5.

❖ **Ish**: the Hebrew name of God, meaning husband. It is used in the books of Hosea, Isaiah, and Jeremiah.

When that day comes," says the Lord, "you will call me 'my husband' instead of 'my master.' I will make you my wife forever, showing you righteousness and justice, unfailing love and compassion. I will be faithful to you and make you mine, and you will finally know me as the Lord. Hosea 2:16, 19-20.

❖ **Abba**: Hebrew name meaning Father.
"He said, "Abba, Father, for you all things are possible; remove this cup from me;yet not what I want, but what you want." Mark 14:36.

❖ **Emmanuel**: means, "God with us."
"Behold, the virgin shall be with child, and bear a Son, and they shall call His name Immanuel," which is translated, "God with us." Matthew 1:22-23.
There is also a name that is above all names. *Yeshua*-God is salvation. God saves. At this name every knee shall bow in heaven and on earth. A combination of the name Yahweh and Yasha meaning rescue or deliver. This personal name given to Jesus attests to God's plan for mankind. It attests to His everlasting and eternal love and grace for His creation. There is immeasurable power in this name.

Points to Ponder

★ *Which of the names or attributes of God resonate with you most?*

★ *How can you apply this attribute to your life at the present moment?*

★ *Can you find other names or attributes of the Creator that resonate with you?*

To pray using the different names of God:

● *Identify a specific name that reflects your current need or situation*

● *Then address God directly using that name, acknowledging the attribute it represents and expressing your prayer accordingly.*

For example:

Call on Yahweh Shalom to minister His peace to you if you feel afraid, worried, dismayed, or perplexed.

Call on Yahweh Rapha if you are sick, and ask for healing.

Call on Yahweh Yireh if you have a pressing need.

Introduction

Shrinking back first occurs in our minds. To shrink back is to pull away from or to withdraw from a source in response to something such as fear. Our beliefs and thoughts become feelings which ultimately leads to the act of shrinking. The result can dramatically affect our life. Constant worry coupled with fear can create dis-ease in life. It can lead to wrong beliefs and negatively impact one's life. Fear thwarts the ability to live an abundant life. We must allow our minds to believe that our Father in Heaven loved us so much, that he gave His Son to give us hope and a more abundant life in spite of circumstances. An abundant life requires belief and trust in Jesus Christ. He must be our central focus. Life is not without challenges or failures, however. As challenges arise, we must choose to face or confront these challenges head on. Avoidance, procrastination, anxiety, fears, and insecurities are all maladaptive behavioral responses that can result from shrinking back.

Adversity and challenges can enrich our faith walk. They can very well draw us closer to the Higher Power and increase our wisdom and understanding. If we align our lives with our Power Source we also embrace divine Truth . We were created to live an abundant life. We were created to represent and model the image of the Divine. "The thief cometh not but for to steal, and to kill, and to destroy: I am come that they might have life and that they might have it MORE ABUNDANTLY" (John 10:10). This abundant life is attainable through belief and knowledge of the wonder working power of God that also works in us.

To live an abundant life we must free ourselves from mental bondage by the power of God. The mental prisons that we create for ourselves are so restraining. There is freedom from fear, stress, anxiety, depression, anger, and insecurities. We can live the life promised to us through the scripture, IF we choose. It is in the scriptures that we find Truth: full sufficiency and provision for what we need is available. We must remind ourselves that our God has big plans for our lives. Do not play small. Do not allow your limiting beliefs to shape your behaviors because it can ultimately shape your life. Life is a journey of highs and lows, good and bad but we can be safeguarded and preserved for what is to come. As a result of growing in relationship with God, trusting and believing in who He says He is, we develop or bear fruits with the help of the Holy Spirit. The fruit of the Spirit manifested is abundance: love, joy, peace, patience, kindness, goodness, faithfulness, gentleness, and self control – manifested when we sincerely seek and study Divine Truths. Abundance and success are ours if our words, thoughts, and behaviors line up with the Word of God. Divine Truth speaks to the promises of those who believe. We fumble the ball when we speak in opposition to the Truth. We must be convinced that we are who God says we are.

The Lord's promises are expressions of His love and care for us. Through them He accomplishes His will and plans for our lives. Our God wants us to prosper in all things as our souls prosper. Our awareness of the truth can be obtained with an earnest heart. SEEK and ye shall find. KNOCK and the door shall be opened for you. It is in the Truth that we are set free; for the Word says: "... you shall know the truth, and the truth shall make you free" (John 8:32). Allow the words of God to untangle the insidious webs of fear, worry, anxiety, and insecurities, BELIEVE, and DO NOT SHRINK BACK.

"For yet in a very little while, He who is coming will come, and will not delay. But my righteous one [the one justified by faith] shall live by faith [respecting man's relationship to God and trusting Him]; And if he draws back [shrinking in fear], My soul has no delight in him. But [a]our way is not that of those who shrink back to destruction, but [we are] of those who believe [relying on God through faith in Jesus Christ, the Messiah] and by this confident faith preserve the soul." (Hebrew 10:37-39 Amp)

OUR DEEPEST FEAR
By Marianne Williamson

Our deepest fear is not that we are inadequate.
Our deepest fear is that we are powerful beyond measure.
It is our light, not our darkness that most frightens us.

We ask ourselves,
"Who am I to be brilliant, gorgeous, talented, fabulous?"
Actually, who are you not to be? You are a child of God.
Your playing small does not serve the world.
There's nothing enlightened about shrinking
so that other people won't feel insecure around you.
We are all meant to shine, as children do.
We were born to make manifest the glory of God
that is within us.

It's not just in some of us; it's in everyone.
And as we let our own light shine, we unconsciously
give other people permission to do the same.
As we're liberated from our own fear,
Our presence automatically liberates others.

"What I feared has come upon me; what I dreaded has happened to me" (Job 3:25).

Chapter I
Fear Not

My story:

The fear of loneliness pierced me. The thought of social isolation and/or singledom ruminated. That thorn, I now know, existed to remind me of my insecurities. These insecurities and low self-esteem plagued me. The negative narrative was conceived and the seeds planted. The seeds of fear would soon catapult me into a constant cycle of negative thinking. Feelings of inadequacy, self doubt, and shame fertilized these seeds.

As a young girl, I would fabricate stories about distant boyfriends to account for the lack of a real and present boyfriend. I had to fit the mold of being in a relationship with a man: the social construct of having a boyfriend to fit in with societal norms was the mold. Fitting the mold would lead to happiness and fulfillment right? Is it the obvious expectation for young women to conform to this societal norm? This pressure to conform may be instinctual. I would daydream, as most young women would, of being whisked away by a heroic male figure. He would rescue me from a fourth-floor walkup and carry me away in a limousine with roses and treats – all this to affirm his love for me. This scene from one of my favorite movies would later skew my vision of love. My fears followed me into high school and college and led to poor decision-making. I settled for what I knew was not what I deserved for the sake of being in a relationship.

Marriage was a fairytale I envisioned all my life. I thought it would quiet my fear of being alone. Get married, have children, and live happily ever after, right? I was pregnant with my second son at the time of our union and saw no signs that the man I was about to marry would ever leave my side. I was very content and happy in the early stages of my marriage despite our differences. We enjoyed spending time together and raising our children in faith. People admired our union. Even though the start and the end of our relationship was difficult, we had great times. We were obviously unequally yoked but managed to enjoy great years together. I recall being fearful of "losing" even during good times.

The seeds of fear were planted and had taken root. I now began to fear being a single mother despite the love and support my ex-husband displayed. He was an overprotective father and a nurturing and loving husband for a time. I would observe single mothers with their children and stare in awe and bewilderment. I would comment, "How do they do it? I could never…" I would think about it, and often say it aloud, not knowing that that would soon be my fate.

My fear imprisoned me. My ability to live fruitfully had been stifled by this fear. As a child, do you remember your parents telling you that they don't have it or affirming, "We are broke?" Well, I was attached to the "We are Broke" anthem. The cycle of repeating, "We are broke" or "We can't afford that" in our household continued. I believe over time that resulted in a scarcity mindset. I affirmed those words without knowing it. The feelings of scarcity loomed over me, ultimately affecting my thoughts and decision-making. I overspent on the things I thought I lacked as a child. I thought I was doing my children a favor by buying the name brands and latest electronics. If I didn't have it, they would. Private school for all four children was a must even if it meant I couldn't afford gas, rent, or groceries. My financial health suffered as a result. Overspending to compensate for the lack in my childhood, to camouflage insecurities or conceal my pain rendered me financially unwell.

The financial strain increased, as I remained the sole provider in our home for years. My empty gas tank could only take me but so far. Thank God for the strangers who would donate gas when asked. My most degrading moments were at the gas station or on the line in the grocery store. Having to walk away from groceries or ask for money to get home from work is a traumatic memory. The sounds of loud, rumbling engines, the hiss of the brakes, and the blaring sounds of trucks when reversing are all still triggering after having my car towed and repossessed – not once but twice. The instinct of running to meet the tower in order to retrieve my personal belongings before losing possession of my car is still fresh in my memory. Bankruptcy, negative balances, and bad credit ensued. Early morning negative-balance text messages plagued me, despite my six-figure salary. My fear had come upon me. Much of what I feared became my reality. It was the script for my screenplay. The life I feared became the life I lived.

Fear has been an enormous stumbling block on my journey. Awareness of the weight of my fear became more evident as I began my Christian walk. While it is a basic human emotion that exists to protect us, it can impede and cripple our faith. Fear is a survival response that can be protective and can also inflict damage on the mind, body, and spirit. It prepares our body for fight or flight by increasing our blood pressure, respirations, and heart rate through the release of chemicals and stress hormones such as cortisol and adrenaline, which are all important for humans when responding to a threat or when in danger.

In lieu of the danger zone, we must listen closely to our thoughts and be attentive to our fears. What do our fears tell us about ourselves? Christians are encouraged to fear not and the reasons are made plain. Does that mean fear is bad? No, It is a human response, but we must not shrink in the face of fear. Awareness is the first step. Then question it and hold the fearful thoughts captive by the eternal Word and power of God. God Himself can quiet our fears as we learn to trust Him.

We can grow in reverential fear of our Heavenly Father by learning how to manage our fears. Surrender through prayer and mindfulness, the use of essential oils, meditation, journaling, or breathing exercises. Spiritual guidance and fellowship are also paramount and can be helpful. Learn to let go and release fear and other emotions that may be harmful. "Put your hands in your pockets" and allow your steps to be guided and controlled by God.

Compelling reasons to banish the spirit of fear can be found throughout the Bible. The Book of Job in the Bible reveals God's wisdom and character in unforeseen circumstances. It also reveals the answers to the question of why there is suffering if God is good. There is no clear answer except the encouragement to trust in God, serve and revere Him through the storms, and in uncertainty. The spirit of fear is not God given – certainly not of God. The scripture asserts that there is no fear in love. God's perfect love can cast out fear.

Can fear be a magnet in attracting the thing we dread the most? Job continually offered sacrifices for the possible sins of his children.

"And it was so, when the days of their fasting were gone about, that Job sent and sanctified them, and rose up early in the morning, and offered burnt offering according to the number of them all: for Job said, It may be that my sons have sinned, and cursed God in their hearts. Thus Job did continually" (Job 1:5). He feared, as mentioned in the word, that his children would curse God in their hearts. It is obvious that Job was a pious man but he also feared. Did Job's fear cause a dismantling of God's hedge of protection? Without this hedge of protection, the enemy, who seeks to destroy and disrupt our lives, has access. We do have the power to resist. The power of the tongue is also worth reviewing. Speaking in the negative is affirming negative. May we trust in God and surrender our fears to Him for He is all sufficient and we must trust that He will continue to meet our every need. For if the lilies of the valley are arrayed with all splendor and beauty how much more shall he clothe us. Let us not be of little faith. Trust and surrender our fears to the Supreme, All-powerful, and All-sufficient One. He will provide! He is faithful.

Reflection:

Let us reflect on the names of God:

The **ELOHIM**-supreme power; **El Shaddai**: the Hebrew name for God, meaning The All-Sufficient One, God Almighty. **Yahweh-Yireh**: the Hebrew name for God – meaning the Lord will provide. The Supreme Power and All-Sufficient One takes my weaknesses and in His sufficiency uses it for His great and mighty purposes. I will focus on the supreme power of God to conquer my fears. I will continue to affirm and believe in His sufficiency, and reflect with gratitude on His provisions for my life.

Scripture:

Philippians 4:19 KJV

"But my God shall supply all your needs according to His riches in glory by Christ Jesus."

1 John 4:18 ESV

"There is no fear in love, but perfect love casts out fear. For fear has to do with punishment, and whoever fears has not been perfected in love."

2 Timothy 1:7 KJV

"For God hath not given us the spirit of fear; but of power, and of love, and of a sound mind."

Isaiah 41:10 NIV

"So do not fear, for I am with you; do not be dismayed, for I am your God. I will strengthen you and help you; I will uphold you with My righteous right hand."

Proverbs 18:20-21 NIV

"From the fruit of their mouth a person's stomach is filled; with the harvest of their lips they are satisfied. The tongue has the power of life and death, and those who love it will eat its fruit."

These scriptures testify of God as ever Faithful and ever Sure.

Poem
"Lord Why Did You Make Me Black"
RuNell Ni Ebo

Lord, Lord

Why did you make me Black?
Why did you make someone
The world wants to hold back?

Black is the color of dirty clothes,
the color of grimy hands and feet.
Black is the color of darkness,
the color of tire-beaten streets.

Why did You give me thick lips,
a broad nose and kinky hair?
Why did You make someone
who receives the hatred stare?

Black is the color of the bruised eye
when someone gets hurt.
Black is the color of darkness,
Black is the color of dirt.

How come my bone structure's so thick,
My hips and cheeks are high?
How come my eyes are brown
and not the color of daylight sky?

Why do people think I'm useless?
How come I feel so used?
Why do some people see my skin
and think I should be abused?

Lord, I just don't understand.
What is it about my skin?
Why do some people want to hate me
and not know the person within?

Black is what people are "listed"
when others want to keep them away.
Black is the color of shadows cast.
Black is the end of day.

Lord you know my own people mistreat me
and I know this just ain't right.
They don't like my hair.
They say I'm too dark or too light.

Lord, don't You think it's time for You
to make a change?
Why don't You re-do creation and
make everyone the same?

God answered:
Why did I make you Black?
Why did I make you Black?
Get off your knees and look around
Tell me, what do you see?
I didn't make you in the image of darkness,
I made you in likeness of ME!

I made you the color of coal from which
beautiful diamonds are formed.
I made you the color of oil,
the black gold that keeps people warm.

I made you from the rich, dark earth that can
grow the food you need.
You color's the same as the black stallion,
a majestic animal is he.
I didn't make you in the image of darkness.
I made you in likeness of ME!

All the colors of the heavenly rainbow can be
found throughout every nation.
But when all of those colors were blended,
you became my greatest creation.

Your hair is the texture of lamb's wool.
Such a humble little creature is he.
I am the Shepherd who watches them.
I am the One who will watch over thee.

You are the color of midnight sky.
I put the star's glitter in your eyes.
There is a smile hidden behind your pain.
That's why your cheeks are so high.

You are the color of dark clouds formed,
when I send My strongest weather.
I made your lips full so when you kiss
the one that you love, they will remember.

Your stature is strong, your bone structure thick
to withstand the burdens of time.
The reflection you see in the mirror…
The image that looks back is MINE.

"I am black but comely, oh ye daughters
of Jerusalem, as the tents of Kedar, as the
curtains of Solomon. Do not stare because I
am darkened by the sun"
(Song of Solomon 1:5-6).

Chapter II

Colorism

Some say, "The blacker the berry, the sweeter the juice," as notably quoted by Tupac. It sure brings my heart great joy to think of my complexion as something that is sweet despite what the world says. The more commonly heard lyrics of the world are, why are you so black? or "stay out the sun. You are too black! If you are darker than this paper bag you don't belong. Marry a white man so your kids will be lighter. They will have better opportunities, A better life…..Colorism is a global pandemic. It is the prejudicial or preferential treatment of an individual of the same ethnicity based on skin color.

My experiences with colorism started early in childhood. Those experiences created a breeding ground for my negative thinking and insecurities. As a child I recall pictures of the other family members (with lighter complexion) on display in the living room of family members' homes. Preferential treatment was obvious. I always wondered why my pictures didn't make it to the breakfront. On one occasion, a family member expressed her disdain after seeing the complexion of my children and realizing that I did not marry a white or lighter skin man. "What did I tell you", she asked. Referring to her request for me to marry a white man when I was a child. The feelings of inadequacy and insecurity would continue to proliferate. My self esteem became deeply affected. I recall making a concerted effort to be around those family members who were much lighter than myself in complexion, in an attempt to be noticed or approved of. I tried so hard to be seen or to be told that I was pretty. I would smile a little harder or people please for validation. As a child, I would pretend to be injured or sick for attention. I would even tell small lies that I thought would cause others to respect me more, or hold me in higher esteem. My cousin constantly reminds me of the stories I would create to seek favor from our grandfather. I would play sick when it was time to do chores and my grandfather would oblige, and have me sit out Saturday morning clean up. These little moments felt like victories and in a strange way fed my ego.

Dating was difficult. My dark skin placed me on the low list of contenders. I did not love the skin I was in. The global standards of beauty set my fate. My childhood and the awareness of society's depiction of beauty fueled my insecurities. Singledom was a norm for a long time. I became used to being the friend that would stand by as her friends got hooked up. Boys often gravitated towards my lighter friends and I often was left standing on the sidelines, alone. "Do you have any other light-skinned friends?" I would hear them ask. I remember a friend's child once asked me why I was so black? I noticed that he was staring at me and somewhat afraid to come close to me, but I was shocked at his question. She turned embarrassingly toward me and apologized. I laughed and shrugged it off as I always did.

Another memorable moment was when a male friend tried to compliment me by saying, "You're pretty for a black girl." I shrunk back in those moments. I could have replied respectfully or with a smart rebuttal, but I didn't. I just placed it in my "shame bucket". The nickname "Blacky" was not fun either. Again, I would laugh it off, but boy, did it sting. I tried hard to quiet my pain but to no avail. Ignorance and social conditioning were to blame – not my family or friends – not the conditioned mind that leads me to believe that the color of my skin defines me. Those experiences caused me to crave acceptance from others and heightened my insecurities. I felt compelled to prove my worth.

The Willie Lynch Letter, written in 1712, sheds light on colorism in a very polarizing way. Though its credibility has been questioned by scholars, this letter describes tactics used by slave masters to set black slaves against each other to maintain control and promote contempt amongst the slaves (en.m.wikipedia.org). It highlights post-slavery tactics used to divide and conquer mind and spirit to divide and destroy people of color. It describes the concerted effort to propagate inferiority and superiority within the race – a tool used to enslave Africans mentally.

In *Willie Lynch letters: The making of a slave,* Lynch (1712) revealed that segregating the black race according to color served as the most effective means by which slave owners could control and manipulate their black slaves. In order to become an effective slave owner, Willie Lynch (1712) argued that "you must use the dark skin slaves vs. the light skin slaves, and the light skin slaves vs. the dark skin slaves. They must love, respect and trust only us…the slaves themselves will remain perpetually distrustful of each other" (Anekwe, 2014). Biased research supported the thought that melanated individuals were inferior and thus justified oppressive efforts ie. the transatlantic slave trade or caste systems. I was better able to understand the depth of colorism after reading the Willie Lynch letter. The effects of colorism are profound and are evident globally with the widespread use of skin lightening products and bleaching creams globally. The debris of self-hatred, injustice, violence, rape, genocide, and war is alarming and immoral.

A hierarchy of human rankings is explained in Isabel Wilkerson's book, *Caste*. She elaborates on the divisions in history and highlights that it is more than just racism. "As we go about our daily lives, Caste is the wordless usher in a dark theater – flashlight cast down in the isles, guiding us to our assigned seats for a performance" (Wilkerson, 2021). It is a deceptive tactic used by the evil one to separate and divide humanity based on a superiority/inferiority system. This has existed from the beginning of time. This tactic has and continues to cause devastation, pain, and sorrow in the lives of many.

Colorism is the design of an evil spirit. It scars, and the wounds run deep. To be belittled and treated unfairly within your race and within families, solely based on your skin tone is disturbing and inhumane. Lisa Victoria Fields describes personhood in her book, *When Faith Disappoints*. She highlights the fact that all our personhood is given by God. Our identity is not limited to our race, to our achievements, to our living situation, or the country that we live in. We are children of the living God. We are made in the identity of Christ. To know and love God is to know and love ourselves. God loves us beyond measure and beyond comprehension. He loves us not because of anything that we have done or how straight our nose is or how light our skin tone is; He loves us because we are made in His image and we are His and He is ours.

The effect of colorism in the United States, the Caribbean, and all across the world is insidious. While there is no one person to blame, we must break the generation cycles of familial oppression. I will not allow the views of society and/or others to affect me. To shrink because my inner child has been bruised is no longer acceptable. I now understand that colorism, racism, discrimination, and caste systems are evil schemes designed to tear down and to destroy. We must not play a part in the enemy's plan to fill our minds with the views of the world. Stand firm on who God says we are.

Our insecurities can leave a stench for the Holy One. A sweet savor to the Lord is to acknowledge, praise, and worship Him. Our lives are a sweet fragrant aroma to God when we devote our lives to Him and walk in love: loving and sacrificing for others, and not counting ourselves better than any other. Do not stare at my skin that is darkened by the SUN (as declared by possibly Queen of Sheba in Song of Songs) but love me as God loves us and His SON. Consider others above yourself. We are all made in the image and likeness of our Creator. My complexion does not make me inferior or superior to you. I am worthy, despite what I face. I am worthy because He calls me worthy. The Word confirms that He chose us in HIM before the foundation of the world, that we should be holy and without blame before Him in love (Eph. 1:4). Christ lives in each and every one of His children: Jew, Gentile, Black, White, Brown – whatever the race, whatever the shade or hue. Let us rejoice and be glad in our creation. Love YOU! Love the creator and His creation. Caste systems don't exist in His kingdom. We are mere reflections of His holiness – no one above another. We are the shades of His rainbow. We are different shades of God's rainbow. We are all precious in His sight.

Reflection:

Let us reflect on one of the names of God:

Qedosh Yisrael is the Hebrew name for God, meaning Holy One of Israel. The Holy One of Israel is a name for God found mostly in the book of Isaiah. He alone is holy and greater than all creation. His greatness is beyond human comprehension. This is where our focus must remain. " I am the Lord, your Holy One, Israel's Creator, your King" (Is 43:15).

Scriptures:

Genesis 1:26-27 NIV

"Then God said, "Let us make mankind in our image, in our likeness, so that they may rule over the fish in the sea and the birds in the sky, over the livestock and all the wild animals, and over all the creatures that move along the ground." So God created mankind in his own image, in the image of God he created them; male and female he created them."

Philippians 2:3 Amp

Do nothing from selfishness or empty conceit [through factional motives, or strife] but with [an attitude of] humility [being neither arrogant nor self righteous], regard others as more important than yourselves."

John 13:34-35 NIV

A new command I give you. Love one another. As I have loved you, so you must love one another. By this everyone will know that you are my disciples, if you love one another.

2 Corinthians 5:17 AMP

Therefore if anyone is in Christ[that is, grafted in, joined to Him by faith in Him as Saviour], he is a new creature [reborn and renewed by the Holy Spirit]; the old things [the previous moral and spiritual condition] have passed away. Behold, new things have come [because spiritual awakening brings a new life].

Galatians 2:20 NKJV

I have been crucified with Christ. It is no longer I who live, but Christ who lives in me; and the life which I now live in the flesh I live by faith in the Son of God, who loved me and gave himself for me.

These scriptures testify of God as Creator and Sustainer.

"Love is patient, love is kind. It does not envy, it does not boast, it is not proud. It does not dishonor others, it is not self-seeking, it is not easily angered, it keeps no record of wrongs. Love does not delight in evil but rejoices with the truth. It always protects, always trusts, always hopes, always perseveres. Love never fails" (1 Corinthians 13:4-8).

Chapter III
Love is Patient; Love is Kind

Relationships:

My first "real" relationship turned into a long-term relationship of about 4 years. We were great friends. Looking back, neither of us was ready for a long-term relationship. Our best friends had started dating and we were both single. With coercion, we eventually became an item. Double dating was fun and exciting. But was I really into him or the idea of having a boyfriend? I was 16 years old, young, and very naive. He lived on the same street as I and we became attached to each other. He eventually joined the Coast Guard. The long distance strained our relationship a bit, despite the weekly correspondence.

During that time I began to learn more about myself. He also questioned the relationship and began to explore other possibilities. I did think we would get married, as did most of our friends and families. I had developed an anxious attachment to him. His desire for me fed the part of me that yearned for acceptance and validation. My desire to have a boyfriend versus a sustainable relationship was unhealthy. I had the unhealthy thought that he was the only person who would see past my complexion and insecurities and maybe the only person who would be interested in me.

Freshman year of college was definitely a time of growth and self-exploration. I met great friends and there I met the father of my children. At the time that we met, he had been a college basketball athlete. As a pre-med major, I spent most of my time socializing with my books in the library. This bookworm would soon become a target for the handsome jock. He was a major flirt and had a girlfriend at the time. That was red flag number one. He was FINE, outgoing, and charming but to my friends he was forbidden. "Don't look in his direction Steph,"my friends would say. My college friends tried to warn me to stay clear of him. They would try to sabotage any attempts to speak with him in the halls. I was reluctant because I wasn't really into jocks, and I knew he would be trouble. The fact that he had a girlfriend was a turn off. He would flirt with me while with her which grossed me out at the time but obviously not enough.

The attention was nice though. I ignored his advances but remained curious until at some point, I noticed that his good looks, his charm, and his sociability seemed to be fading. He was dressed in sackcloth. Yes, sackcloth like the potato bags. He and his girlfriend were no longer together and his beautiful yet mischievous smile disappeared. It soon became known that he had lost his adopted father in a car accident and was having a hard time dealing with the loss. I began to fixate on him and became interested in helping. The Florence Nightingale in me was activated: solving and fixing him became my mission and project.

My first boyfriend was coming back around and was now stationed in New York, but he had lost my interest. I had a new project to work on – a mysterious, handsome but troubled project. Upon his return home, I had bigger questions for him about life and spirituality. Our conversations were empty and many of my questions unanswered. I would ask him about his passions and dreams. I would ask questions such as: Do you believe in God? Do you pray? Where do you see yourself in the future? Career…? He couldn't answer any of my questions. He eventually became aware that my mind was elsewhere, and one morning left a box with a letter folded in the shape of a ring inside the small box, with what I believe was a proposal. Of course, this went unnoticed and the relationship soon ended.

The relationship between my ex-husband and I evolved and we started on a spiritual journey together. The Bible study journey between the two of us yielded a strong physical and emotional attraction. Our conversations were different. He was very different. We had really deep conversations about life and God. I then met a friend of his who would hang out on campus. Our meetups included history lessons and Bible reading. Late nights in his mom's apartment turned into overnight stays. There was an excitement and a thrill in getting to know this man. He had a bad boy edge that was appealing to me.

Looking back I do see how I shrunk back. I knew to my core that we were not compatible. The deeper and deeper we dove into the Torah, the more excited I became – the more I wanted to share these truths with others. I would run home after spending hours reading scripture to share what I learned with my family. I began spending more time at the temple on Sabbaths. When I started to wrap up my hair, that's when my parents became concerned. All hell broke loose, once I became pregnant. My Caribbean parents were devastated. I was not married and I was in my third year of college, with no degree, no job, no place to live. The shroud of disappointment and pain on my parents was heavy. They didn't look at me or touch me for months during my pregnancy. My mother mourned bitterly and I didn't understand why.

We were in love. He supported me throughout my years of pursuing my education. He was there to transport me to and from work. He was there to raise our children, cook, and clean. He attempted to perfect frying dumplings and preparing rice and peas. He tried so hard to make it as close to my father's as possible because of how much we all loved my father's dumplings and rice and peas. He would often comment about the close knit family unit I had. He would refer to us as the Huxtables. He tried hard to measure up to the "Huxtables". His childhood trauma scars were deep. Despite his adoption into a loving family, his pain remained. His unresolved trauma soon turned to anger and resentment towards those that loved him most – his wife and children.

It was early into the alcohol addiction and after the birth of our fourth child that the idea of a second wife came about. Because this was welcomed in the culture, most thought that it would be a great idea. A few of the females tried convincing me that it would be ideal for our family. He had already chosen the young lady and she was definitely interested. I strongly opposed the idea and made this clear very early into our relationship, not knowing I would have to revisit this later in my marriage. The more divided we became on this matter the more the drinking intensified. I spoke with the young lady and informed her that anything I did not consent to was adultery and would not stand for it. She and her family soon became aware of my views. He also understood that I would walk out the door with the children if it continued. Our relationship was never the same after that . Our finances were strained and the addition of another child was stressful. I was the sole provider for many years and the idea of welcoming a second wife reared its head before the conception of our last and fourth child.

It was hard to accept this reality. How could someone who hated the taste of alcohol become addicted to it? My initial denial of his addiction was damaging to our family. To be quite honest his addiction existed way before he could make sense of what addiction was. What was obvious was the addiction to sex, marijuana, and women. What was I to do? Alcohol bottles lined the kitchen counter. I was afraid to admit that there was a problem. I must admit that I did shrink in those moments. My thoughts were: *Maybe it would go away on its own. Maybe no one would notice. It can't be that bad.* When confronted he would deny that there was a problem, of course. "I can stop when I want to," he would say. Ironically, I started a job at an addiction treatment center at the time: a learning curve on the nature of addiction, to say the least. His addiction turned him into someone we no longer recognized. His closest family members were in disbelief. We prayed that he would not succumb to the pain, but would emerge out of darkness stronger than ever, with an amazing testimony: proclaiming and professing the love of the Creator and recognizing the testament of His son. This remains our prayer. Love always hopes and always perseveres.

The love of God transcends all. The eternal love was brought forth through Christ Jesus. This was planned before the beginning of time. Our Creator knew that we were incapable of loving within the confines of our human minds, so He provided a perfect example of sacrificial love. We know love because He first loved us. His love is eternal and is the model of how we as humans should love others. Love is a decision. We decide to serve and give. My number one supporters are my parents. Dad's love is what gives me my resilience. The love and sacrifices of my parents have been my foundation. I recall, when I was in school, days of being sent home from school for lack of tuition payment. As I think of the sacrifices they made to provide a private education and housing for my brother and I on a small budget, my heart is filled with gratitude.

Love is patient. My parents were kind enough to have my husband move in with us after leaving our home. We moved most of our belongings into storage and took up occupancy in my parents' home. They were very leery of having him stay with us, given his years of heavy drinking and being in and out of emergency rooms. My parents loved my ex-husband, the father of their grandchildren, and wanted desperately for him to heal and recover from his addiction. The first few months were unnerving. Was he able to quit drinking on his own as he promised? My father actually was the one who came to me and said that he no longer could stay there with us. He had been sleeping throughout the day and neglecting the children. The kids would watch him sleep while in his drunken stupor. He obviously was just not willing to seek the help and commit to being better. So we eventually had to call 911 and EMS to have him leave the premises. He refused to leave and I remember my father actually crying. I knew at that point that I could no longer shrink back; I could no longer engage with him unless he recognized that he needed help and showed signs of truly being committed to getting better. Love is holding others accountable to change, especially when their lifestyle is harmful to themselves and others.

I made up my mind that night. After pleading with my ex to get into an ambulance to get the help he needed, he ran away from the EMS crew and never set foot in my parents home again. After jumping out of the ambulance, he would later call and badger me. "How could you throw me out?" he would text. He would come to the house in the early hours of the morning and tap on the windows of the basement, where my nephew and sister were staying temporarily, to ask for a blanket and other miscellaneous things. Could I have done anything more to help him? Could I have loved the pain, depression, anxiety, addiction, and childhood trauma out of him?

I reminded myself that I was not responsible for anyone's healing. I was not responsible for his recovery. I will always love the father of my children. I continue to love him despite having no contact with him. I will continue to hope that he will be an active participant in helping himself to become well. We each have a part to play and we have to have the desire to be better, to work through the mental and emotional constraints that limit us. Thinking that I could fix him or change him or love him out of his pain was delusional and caused me to shrink in the face of what I knew to be wrong.

Being wanted or being chosen equated to worthiness, and validated my very existence. I craved validation romantically, professionally, personally, and spiritually; not recognizing that the ultimate source of validation is God. The body of Christ is another source for healthy validation in the context of building one another up . Love is patient and love is kind. "I love you Stephanie." I am reminded through this scripture to nurture, love, and be kind to myself despite and inspite of all the storms of life. In order to effectively love others and extend grace and mercy, I must apply it to myself. I must reflect the love of God and will continue to challenge myself to mirror this love. I dated my first boyfriend and didn't really have another serious relationship aside from my husband since the age of 16. I was uncomfortably alone and I found myself in situations that were not acceptable or safe. I threw myself into these situations to physically fill a void that only God can fill. I was always reaching for something to fill me, to make me better, or to validate me. No man or degree, no amount of money or job, skin complexion or length of hair, or shape of body can validate me. My worth lies with the Creator.

The love of God transcends all. The eternal love was brought forth through Christ Jesus. This was planned before the beginning of time. Our Creator knew that we were incapable of loving within the confines of our human minds, so He provided a perfect example of sacrificial love. We know love because He first loved us. His love is eternal and is the pinnacle for how we as humans should love others. The love of God has been poured out within our hearts through the Holy Spirit. Most often, the word "compassion" and the deep emotion it conveys is associated with God. The Bible gives many examples of God's love and compassion – as a parent, a father, a husband, and even as a nursing mother. Our relationship with God is life sustaining. The marriage to the bridegroom of Christ is our destiny and unites us in spirit: the Creator of Heaven and Earth. It is from this union that all relationships are modeled. It is also with this union that we have salvation and unity with God. By far this may be the greatest love story ever told.

Reflection:

Let us reflect on one of the names of God.
Ish is the Hebrew name of God, meaning husband.

Our most important relationship is our relationship with God – our knowledge of God's love. You are worthy. Don't settle. Know when you are not invited to sit at the table and WALK AWAY, if you are not. Love as Jesus does – freely, without reciprocity, and with healthy boundaries. "By this everyone will know that you are my disciples, if you love one another" (John 13:35).

Scriptures:

1 John 3:1 ESV

"See what kind of love the Father has given us, that we should be called children of God; and so we are."

1 John 4:9-10; 16-19 KJV

"In this was manifested the love of God toward us, because that God sent his only begotten Son into the world, that we might live through him. Herein is love, not that we loved God, but that he loved us, and sent his son to be the propitiation of our sins. And we have known and believed the love that God hath to us. God is love; and he that dwelleth in love dwelleth in God, and God in him. Herein is our love made perfect, that we may have boldness on the day of judgment: because as he is, so are we. There is no fear in love; but perfect love casteth out fear; because fear hath torment. He that feareth is not made perfect in love. WE LOVE HIM, BECAUSE HE FIRST LOVED US."

These scriptures testify of God as LOVE.

"The thief comes only to steal and kill and destroy; I have come that they may have life, and have it to the full." John 10:10

Chapter IV
They Will Be Ok

The thought of swerving my car off the road on the highway, or of driving into oncoming traffic bombarded my thoughts often. I rehearsed it in my mind. No one would ever know. I had no clinical diagnosis nor did anyone know how much I struggled to cope with what happened. The immensity of the pain seemed too much to bear. As a newly single mom with four kids, living in my parents home was an enormous sense of embarrassment, defeat, and failure. Feelings of despair and inadequacy, anger, and rage gripped me. I felt unworthy. I was emotionally, financially, psychological, and spiritually unwell. I didn't share these thoughts with anyone.

My psychological pain began to torment me. It would be deemed an accident and my children would be secure financially. I made sure to maximize the life insurance benefits to afford them a better life. They would have the love of their grandparents to sustain them. I would be able to permanently sleep the pain away. The pain I experienced was unbearable. What made it worse was that I bottled it all up. I chose to retain the harmful fragments of loss, betrayal, embarrassment, and disappointment within my core. I shrunk in my pain. I dressed my sorrow up with a beautiful bow and fancy wrapping. I was a well dressed mess. A doctor in distress. "Are you the only one in pain, Stephanie?" What a trail of debris that would be left behind for my family – particularly my children. My children! My gifts from the Most High God! The thought of abandoning them was unsettling. I challenged my thoughts and tried to focus on the positives. I sought God fervently in prayer, stayed the course, and chose life. I choose to live.

I abandoned myself when I thought of taking my life. I tried navigating life while living with my parents, my brother, sister, nephew, and my four children, but I couldn't help feeling like a failure. I could only think that My decisions were the cause of our duress. Why didn't I take heed to the warning signs? Why was I not able to fix this all? My ex husband was now MIA (missing in action) after stints in rehab and group homes. I continued to question life and faith; I also questioned God's purpose for my life. What did I ever do to deserve this? I prided myself on being "a good girl" all my life. My mom would remind me that she told me that this would happen, shortly after meeting my betrothed. "You didn't want to listen, Steph. I knew you weren't a good match," others would say. "What were you thinking?" I put up a great front as I struggled to move past the pain. Or, at least I thought I did.

My bed became a river at night. It was a place of cathartic release and comfort. It was where I could be honest with my feelings. I was free in those moments of anguish. Nights were long and silent; dark and lonely but my moments of release happened in my riverbed of prayers and tears. I eventually found solace in the river of tears. The façade that was built during the day was dismantled at night.

I learned to busy myself to mask the pain. I worked two jobs and had started my doctoral degree one year after moving in with my parents. I remember being so disappointed in the fact that I didn't start the year prior, despite the fact that I had just gone through one of the most painful moments of my life. I became employed at a reputable

Hospital in New York and attended my alma mata for doctoral studies. I found joy in my career and in helping others. It was by the grace of God that I was able to care for my patients and children while neglecting my psychological, physical, and spiritual needs. I was a pretty, assembled mess. I was "selling health and wellness but not buying it". Embarrassment and shame enveloped me, and my spirit became broken as I tried to ignore the immense pain and feelings of abandonment.

He has created us to live life and to live life more abundantly – CHOOSE LIFE. Fear not of the terror by night nor the arrow that flieth by day: Nor the pestilence that walks in darkness. Nor the destruction that wastes at noonday. (Ps 91:5-6). True reliance on God through faith in Jesus Christ is my saving grace and can be yours as well. He has not left you or forsaken you. He sees us. He bears witness to our struggles and our trials. Like Hagar in the Bible, He sees YOU. Hagar was considered an outcast, an Egyptian . She ran away after being mistreated by Sarai. The angel of the Lord visits her at a well. Gen 16:13, "Then she called the name of the Lord who spoke to her, *You are God who sees*, for she said, "Have I not even here {in the wilderness} remained alive after seeing Him { who sees me with understanding and compassion}?" I am confident in You and will depend on You in spite of the pain."

"Seeing "it" as personal diminishes your power over it, your understanding. How quickly your mind defines abandonment as a signature of your unworthiness. Unworthiness does NOT exist. It is an idea we pass around. A feeling that weeds itself up in our crevasses. You cannot exist and not be worthy. Worthy of healing, of being a whole, reckoning, relating human being."
– J. John 157

Reflection:

Let us reflect on the names of God:

El Roi: the Hebrew name for God, meaning the God who sees me. **Yahweh Tsuri** -the Lord is my rock. Fear not; shrink not. Rely on God through faith in Jesus Christ.

Scriptures:

Isaiah 40:31 Amp

"But those who wait for the LORD [who expect, look for, and hope in Him] Will gain new strength and renew their power; They will lift up their wings [and rise up close to God] like eagles [rising toward the sun]; They will run and not become weary, They will walk and not grow tired."

No More Smalling Up of Me
By Jean Wilson

No more meekly saying yes when my heart is screaming No.
No more taming of my feelings so my power won't show no more.
Hiding my exuberance from disapproving eyes
No more watering down myself so my spirit won't rise.
No more smalling up of me, pretending I'm not here.
No more running from the music in the spotlight's glare
No more living in this prison, barricaded by my fears.
No more turning and retreating in the face of new frontiers.
Even as I'm speaking I'm taking a shape and form.
Harnessing my power is like a gathering store.
There's no obstacle so bold as to do your stand in my way.
I'm taking back my life and I'm doing it today.
No more smalling up of me.

"Like arrows in the hands of warriors are children born in one's youth. Blessed is the man whose quiver is full of them".
(Psalm 127:5).

Chapter V
The Fruit of My Womb

"Becoming a mother leaves no woman as it found her. It unravels her and rebuilds her. It cracks her open, takes her to her edges. It's both beautiful and brutal; often at the same time.
        – Nikki McCahon.

"Why would anyone want to have four children in this day and age," said a well-known children's author who I cared for during my days while working in the ICU. I remembered sharing with him that my children loved his books, and to my surprise he despised children – go figure. I always wanted a big family and was so excited to be a mother. Babies number three and four were not planned but very much welcomed. I had uncomplicated pregnancies and enjoyed being pregnant. How magical is it to know that there is life growing inside your womb. Besides baby colic and longer than usual breastfeeding, all went well. My children were natural born except for the first born. Each birthing experience was enriching and were memorable experiences.

The birthing process is one of the most humbling experiences I have ever gone through. I was at the helm of my body, trusting in God for a smooth delivery each time. The ability to assist in bringing forth life in this world is an amazing gift. I am not sure how to accurately describe this honor. Though we may travail in pain while giving birth, it is the most priceless gift – to assist in bringing forth life. It is an overwhelming love that empowers and humbles you.

I acknowledge the fruits of my womb as a precious gift. The womb is the source of life. It is where God knits our human form into a woven image of himself. A Hebrew word which translates to compassion, mercy, and love in the scriptures is the word Racham. The root of this word also means womb. It conveys the deep love, compassion, and mercy of our God for his children and of a parent for their child. How wonderful is it that God uses this very word to describe his character. In Isaiah 49:15-16 God said, "Can a woman forget her nursing child and have no compassion? ...I will not forget, saith the Lord. God's love is tender and compassionate. An unyielding and unrelenting outburst of emotion that endures forever. He loves us as deeply as a mother/parent loves their child.

My firstborn was dedicated to the Lord in prayer. I promised to keep him in the word and in a house of prayer as was necessary for all my children. His name means "gift of God". A gift from God that I am forever grateful for. You are a leader, very organized, wise, conscientious, and very determined. I recall our first night alone in the hospital room. His big eyes staring at me in the darkness of the night was unnerving. While I was excited to finally meet the child that was housed in my womb, I questioned if I was ready to be a mother. We held a "redemption ceremony" for our first born at the age of one. Our family members were perplexed and wondered why I didn't go through with a regular church baptism. They supported us nonetheless. Under a canopy in my parents' backyard, the drummers from our temple played as we read the scriptures pertaining to the ceremonial tradition of redeeming the first-born son. The children's father presented our first born to a priest/Levite, which symbolized returning his firstborn to God. Coins were then offered to the priest in place of the child and upon acceptance of payment, the son is redeemed. The father is in essence buying his son from the priest to redeem him. This ceremonial act is reminiscent of the promise of God to deliver us from the power and presence of sin with the birth, life, and death of Jesus Christ. God so loved the world that he sent his son to redeem each individual who puts his or her faith in Him.

Each of my sons had circumcisions done on the 8th day of life as we believed was commanded of us. The first experience was unpleasant for me for a few reasons: I was not able to be present due to religious law regarding "cleanliness after childbirth". Based on Levitical law, the female was not to enter the temple until 40 days after giving birth to a son, and 80 days for a female as denoted in the book of Leviticus. My postpartum confinement from the temple was also a source of debate for months after the procedure. The circumcision was done incorrectly and needed to be corrected. A professional mohel did the next two circumcisions. The mohel, or man trained in the practice of brit milah or the covenant of circumcision, came to our home to perform the procedure. I was very much present for it. While unconventional, it was an intimate and very memorable experience.

Our second born is a ball of energy. He is compassionate, kind, and intuitive. He weighed 7 lbs, 11 ounces at birth when he made his entrance at 1:30 am. His birth was unusual in that the amniotic sac was intact when delivered. The midwife explained how rare this was and shared her knowledge of the meaning of this. A journal entry one month after his birth, details his fiery personality. The transition from one to two children was the hardest for me. There was a sense of guilt and overwhelmingness. I was super conscious of the need to balance my time between both children. I was concerned for my oldest child. I wondered if it was possible to provide for both without short changing the other. I also wondered if my first born would feel neglected or abandoned as I nurtured his little brother?

The birth of our princess was refreshing, but it was my most painful birthing experience. She was born at 3:37 am weighing 7lbs, 10 oz. The thought of having a daughter after the birth of my sons was exciting for my ex-husband and I. Her father was pleased to name her. He took his time – choosing a name with a powerful meaning. Her Hebrew name means, Nation of God. I named our 2 sons with Hebrew names as well. Our daughter is a beautiful young lady with a feisty but tempered personality. She exudes femininity, grace and beauty, along with intelligence and wisdom. My goal is to continue to affirm her with the words of the scripture. "Society will place no value on you," I declared to her.

Our strong willed last born son was a pleasant surprise. He was delivered by my hands in a birth tub with his siblings and father around me. He was my most beautiful and memorable birthing experience. He came in weighing almost 9 lbs, 15 minutes after I arrived at the birthing center. He was born at a time when I began to question spiritual and relational connections. Things became clearer for me after his birth. He had intense mood swings and frequent crying spells as a baby. We were very uncertain of the cause at that time but it soon became clearer. He is a beautiful child – artistic, insightful, confident, and smart.

I didn't know what the impact of my firstborn going off to college would be. I mourned the first year but the temporary separation became less and less painful. My second son is now more than 800 miles away and I am filled with mixed emotions. Oh, the joy and the pain all at the same time. I miss them so much but I gain comfort knowing that they will return. The cycle will continue as they marry or move away, I am sure. I again lean on the Father to guide them as they mature and venture out into the world. Each of my children is athletic and intuitive. Our first-born's independence and maturity is refreshing. He is introverted, practical, and a leader. The middle child is the compassionate, charismatic, confident extrovert. The last born is artistic, sensitive, but a fearless teenager. The princess embraces her femininity. She is radiant, intelligent, kind, but stern.

As their stories unfold, I am brought closer to God. They continue to teach me the art of patience and forgiveness, and how to love unconditionally. Each of their personalities is so unique. God has created them so beautifully and fearfully. Learning how to parent each personality type has been an exercise without saying. I continue to discover more about myself as I witness each of them evolve. As my sons and daughter navigate life without the presence of their father, my spirit aches. Every birthday and graduation, and milestone comes with both joy and grief. I grieve the lack of a healthy father figure in their lives. However, I understand that God's favors and protection may have meant his absence was necessary. At pivotal moments in life, I sense their frustration in not having an earthly father to validate and affirm them. The father-child relationship is a gift from the Lord. The absence of their earthly father will forever leave a void that only our heavenly Father so graciously can fill. I rest in the comfort that God is their Father. He will never leave or forsake them. My prayer is that they go forth, seek, and find Him.

Message for my children: I have never known a love like this. A love that constantly challenges me to be better and to never give up. A love that forces me to stand in the face of uncertainty, to stand and face challenges, and to stand on the word of God. As I stand, I pray that you are encouraged to do the same in life. The role of a parent is an extension of God's love for his children. His love is unconditional and unwavering.

A Mother's Prayer

Jesus, above all else I ask that you would call my children to yourself and that nothing would hinder them from coming to you (Matthew 19:14). May they confess with their mouths, You as Lord, Jesus, and believe in their hearts that God raised You from the dead (Romans 10:9). Let Your Word richly dwell within them, Father (Colossians 3:16), and even as they grow in knowledge and understanding I pray that they will never lose their childlike faith (Luke. 18:17).

Lord, let our children know and embrace the magnitude of Your love (Ephesian 3:18) and the freedom of Your grace (Romans 6:14), learning daily to walk and be empowered by the Spirit and not to carry out the desires of their flesh (Ephesian 3:16; Gal. 5:16). Teach them to actively submit to you, to be quick to confess and forsake their sin, and to resist the devil so he will flee from them (Proverbs 28:13; James 4:7). As they turn from evil, let them cling to You, love You, and hunger and thirst for righteousness (Joshua 23:8,11; Matt. 5:6), and in so doing may they obey You (1 John 1:3) and bear fruit so that Your joy may be in them, Jesus (John 15:10-11).

Help them also to honor us, their parents, by obeying us in Your name (Ephesians 6:1-2). Today and always, I pray our children will be kind, tender-hearted and forgiving toward one another and others (Ephesian 4:32), and may they regard each other and all others as more important than themselves (Philippians 2:3). Surround our children with wise, God-fearing peers and mentors who will help us teach and demonstrate for them how to seek wisdom, listen to counsel and walk in integrity (Proverbs 8:17, 12:15, 10:9). Keep their minds pure, desiring and dwelling on all things good and praiseworthy (Philippians 4:8) and overflowing with gratitude (Colossians 2:7).

Finally, incline our children's hearts, Lord God, to pray in all things (Ephesians 6:18; Phil. 4:6; 1 Thessalonians. 5:17; Jam. 5:13-16). Grant us the greatest joy, Father, by allowing us to see our children walking in the Truth (3 John 1:4). We give you all praise and glory, Lord, for all the work You have done and will do in our children's hearts and lives.

Amen.

But from everlasting to everlasting the Lord's love is with those who fear him, and his righteousness with their children's children. – Psalm 103:17

By Lisa Goodin, 2015.

Reflection:

Let us reflect on the names of God:

Miqweh Yisrael is the Hebrew name for God, meaning Hope of Israel.

"O Lord, you alone are my hope. I've trusted you, O Lord, from childhood."

(Psalm 71:5). **El Shaddai**: the Hebrew name for God, meaning The All-Sufficient One, God Almighty. Abba: Father. Only mentioned three times in the Bible: Romans 8:15, Galatians 4:6, and Mark 14:36. God is our heavenly Father. Our Father hears us: "Which of you, if your son asks for bread, will give him a stone? Or if he asks for a fish, will give him a snake? If you, then, though are evil, know how to give good gifts to your children, how much more will your Father in heaven give good gifts to those who ask Him!" (Matthew 7:9-11)

Scriptures:

Jeremiah 1:5 (NKJV)

"Before I formed you in the womb I knew you; Before you were born I sanctified you; I ordained you a prophet to the nations."

Psalm 139:13-16 (AMP)

"For you formed my inward parts; you knit me together in my mother's womb. I praise you, for I am fearfully and wonderfully made. Wonderful are your works; my soul knows it very well. My frame was not hidden from you, when I was being made in secret, intricately woven in the depths of the earth.

2 Corinthians 6:15-18 (KJV)

"And what agreement hath the temple of God with idols? for ye are the temple of the living God; as God hath said, I will dwell in them, and walk in them; and I will be their God, and they shall be my people. Wherefore come out from among them, and be ye separate, saith the Lord, and touch not the unclean thing; and I will receive you. And will be a Father unto you, and ye shall be my sons and daughters, saith the Lord Almighty."

Ephesians 1:7 (NIV)

"In Him we have redemption through his blood, the forgiveness of sins, in accordance with the riches of God's grace."

Isaiah 44:22 (NLT)

"I have swept away your sins like a cloud. I have scattered your offenses like the morning mist. Oh, return to me, for I have paid the price to set you free."

Psalm 107:2-6 (NIV)

"Let the redeemed of the Lord tell their story – those he redeemed from the hand of the foe – those he gathered from the lands, from east and west, from north and south. Some wandered in desert wastelands, finding no way to a city where they could settle. They were hungry and thirsty, and their lives ebbed away. Then they cried out to the Lord in their trouble, and he delivered them from their distress."

These scriptures testify of the Lord as Redeemer.

"The Lord said to Moses, tell Aaron and his sons, this is how you are to bless the Israelites. Say to them, The Lord bless you and keep you. The Lord make his face shine on you and be gracious to you. The Lord turn his face toward you and give you peace. So they will put my name on the Israelites and I will bless them."
(Numbers 6:22-27)

Chapter VI
The Levitical Prayer

Much of my spiritual foundation developed while attending Catholic school from preschool to college. I learned of Jesus and God and much about Catholicism without much understanding. Memorization of prayers and songs during my formative years helped to develop my moral compass. Our elementary school did a good job at having us memorize the Beatitudes and the 10 Commandments year after year. These things slowly became ingrained in our minds – with the mandatory masses – with the pomp and circumstance of the Catholic Church. The smell of frankincense, the confessional booths, and the lines for communion are vivid memories. I revered the ceremonial traditions not understanding the meaning. I desperately wanted to join the communion lines. I felt alienated being left behind by most of my classmates in the pew. I made my way to the line once or twice without notice and took part in communion as a non-Catholic. How did the bread and the blood of Christ equate to eating a matzo cracker and drinking grape juice? Why am I not able to partake of this? I wondered. What did it all mean? I did not have the answer to those questions then.

I have been blessed to be surrounded by very spiritual and intuitive individuals, one of whom is my step-grandmother. She is a

Seventh-day Adventist and as children we observed the Sabbath day with her. I recall my brother, my cousins, and I sitting on the floor with her as she read through Scriptures. She often fasted and appeared to be in deep union with her Creator. The desire and reverence was within me. I remember focusing on the words she read us and visualizing the biblical stories she shared. She was so passionate and dedicated to worship. Her love for God was intriguing even at a young age. I desired that connection. I remember hearing my mom speak of her disdain for denominations and of the theatrics of communion in some churches. My parents believed in a higher power. We wore our crucifixes regularly and would make an effort to attend services on holidays such as Easter: dad would usually chauffeur us to the services. Attending one or two services in the year was strongly encouraged by our mother. Throughout high school and college, I remained faithful but questions became concerns, and college became the time for questioning and exploration.

Years were spent blaspheming the name of Yeshua, denying his very existence; I questioned the accuracy and authenticity of the New Testament and refused to read it. Torah's filled our home and replaced the King James Bibles that we owned. The name Jesus deliberately was not mentioned. We would refer to Him as J.C. or occasionally Yeshua. We were taught that Jesus was a mere prophet that may have existed in history. My ex-husband and I would go on self appointed outreach missions to local churches on Sunday mornings and would walk in with a staff. Yes, a long staff, and addressed the ministers with questions. As I stood by his side, he would challenge the ministers and congregants, imploring them to stop idolizing and worshiping false gods – referencing Jesus. These moments were uncomfortable and embarrassing at times. We oftentimes were escorted out of these places of worship. The goal was to seek righteousness and to speak truth and open the eyes of the idolaters.

As an Israelite, there was this sense of pride as a dark skinned woman living in America with Jamaican ancestry. It can be somewhat daunting (as a person of color), to exist in a whitewashed world even though things have changed a bit with natural women embracing their natural hair, and are now gracing the covers of magazines and TV shows. We have had our first male black president. There is now a sense of pride in whom we are created to be. People of color are now embracing their hues and shapes and kinks and curls despite the more common vision was that of very fair skinned, blond haired, and blue-eyed individuals. We have been made to believe for so long that this is the epitome of beauty. So sitting in the temple, reading scripture, and imagining myself as a direct descendent of Sarai, Queen Esther, Rebecca, or Deborah gave me a sense of worth. I felt a sense of belonging as I probed through the scriptures and embraced the idea that the Hebrew Israelites may very well have looked like me.

The narrative changed. The white Jesus that I stared at for years in churches and on TV screens may not have been blue eyed with blonde hair. He may have had long locks and dark skin. "But, Stephanie, does that matter?" some may ask. Representation matters. Why is it that people of color have been viewed as second class for centuries? Why is most of the history of individuals of color diluted or not highlighted? Why is it that we are the most hated race on this entire planet? Why are we the tail and not the head in most respects? These questions haunted me.

My ex-husband and I started studying scripture with friends, and journeyed towards what we called, "the truth" at that time. Our truth was found only in the Old Testament. And we spent hours and days and years combing through the Old Testament, combing through scripture, oftentimes debating scripture. And we also had moments of joy and warmth and fulfillment. The Hebrew Israelite temple was our home for many years. This temple was very small, found in a not so nice part of town, but was so inviting. The smell of frankincense and myrrh, the warmth, the energy, the drums, the music, the devotion, the prayers, the singing, and the laughter of all the children were delightful.

Sabbath days were long, but sweet and warm. The smell of incense and the sound of drums with women, men, and children singing, praying, laughing, and rejoicing were invigorating. There was a manner in which we entered the sanctuary and how we departed. We entered backwards in reverence to the Most High God. Our heads were covered. Men and women sat on opposite sides of the room. Shoes were off and our attention was on exploring the Old Testament with the Moreh (teacher) and listening to the message for the day, with musical interludes. The elders usually sat in the first 2 rows in the sanctuary. They were filled with advice, wisdom and strengths. I always felt so comfortable sitting next to them. Dinner was often shared amongst the congregation and by sundown we would make our way home. The voice of one of the sisters remains in my memory. One sister's rendition of this Psalm reeked of pain, longing, despair, and expectation. It remains forever etched in my heart. I connected with the longing in her voice when she sang Psalm 137.

Psalms 137:1-6 KJV

"By the rivers of Babylon, there we sat down, yea, we wept, when we remembered Zion. We hanged our harps upon the willows in the midst thereof. For there they that carried us away captive required of us a song; and they that wasted us required of us mirth, saying, sing us one of the songs of Zion. How shall we sing the Lord's song in a strange land? If I forget thee, O Jerusalem, let my right hand forget her cunning. If I do not remember thee, let my tongue cleave to the roof of my mouth; If I prefer not Jerusalem above my chief joy."

The focus on captivity and being under the curse puzzled me. We are in captivity because of our sins, we were told. We are the tail and not the head because we have not obeyed the laws of the Torah. We are an arrogant nation of people hence why we are made to be the tail in most parts of the world. While there are still things that I hold true regarding the Hebrew Israelite culture, I am aware of the danger of a few of the cultures philosophies. I'm aware of how it can lead us away from the ultimate truth and lead us to focus on genealogy and race. The laws of the Torah binds. Polygamy was a sensitive topic for many, but it was accepted. I became rigid and was held in bondage to the laws that were impossible to keep. There was a level of self-righteousness. The truth of the gospel is absent, and focus on the 364 laws caused inner turmoil. There were also intrapersonal conflicts and disagreements among my family, friends, and eventually between my ex-husband and me.

My time in fellowship with the Hebrew Israelites was life changing, nonetheless. I now recognize that the journey was necessary and it has augmented my Christian walk. It was uplifting, enlightening, and empowering. The Hebrew Israelite camp encouraged us to view ourselves as the chosen people, as possibly one of the lost tribes of Israel. The culture encouraged knowledge of self and resistance to society's representation of people of color. Our responsibility was to obey the hundreds of commands in the Old Testament. My ex-husband was very zealous. It was actually shocking to see his transformation from that college jock to that pious Levite. The elders of the temple, due to his obedience, passion, and zeal, had referred to him as a Levite. He on occasion would minister to the congregation and was determined to be obedient to the written law.

The piety and righteousness that developed in my ex-husband was refreshing and very attractive. I witnessed his love for scripture and for his Israelite brothers and sisters. The more he studied scripture the more confident and zealous he became. He taught himself the Hebrew language and studied for hours daily. Over the course of several years, I noticed that his light began to diminish. I also felt as though something was missing. Studying scripture and congregating with the family was always a blessing. The truth found in scripture is what it is – truth, but the context was misunderstood. My spirit became perplexed. Changes became evident in my ex-husband when we saw inconsistencies with what we were being taught – inconsistencies within the congregation. Polygamy tore some families apart. The missing piece is Jesus. God has saved us and has freed us from the "curse of the law". There had to be more to the Levitical story.

Who are the chosen people? Many groups throughout history have considered themselves to be the chosen people. The scriptures are very clear in highlighting that the Israelites were chosen by God.

"Now if you obey me fully and keep my covenant, then out of all nations you will be my treasured possession" (Exodus 19:5). "Although the whole earth is mine, you will be for me a kingdom of priests and a holy nation" (Exodus 19:6). When we join these early followers of Jesus in inviting others into the story of God's love for all people, we are also living out our identity as God's chosen people – those whose special purpose has always been to extend God's inclusive love to many. Israel's role is to reconcile all the nations to Yahweh. Israel is meant to faithfully represent God by how they live as a community of love, justice, and worship of Yahweh alone. This is what the law is all about. Israel is chosen not for salvation, but for a purpose. They are called to display who Yahweh is to all the nations, so that all would come to know and worship the one true God. The Israelites in the scripture stand as a literal and metaphorical symbolism of the covenant people or believers of Christ. Salvation to the nations was God's mission all along (2019).

Reflection:

Let us reflect on one of the names of God:

Yahweh: the Hebrew name for God meaning, I Am, The Self-Existent One. I Am – He was – He is. He always has been and always will be. He is the Self-Existent One with no beginning and no end. God replied to Moses, "I am who I am. Say this to the people of Israel: "I Am" has sent me to you." God also said to Moses, "Say this to the people of Israel: Yahweh, the God of your ancestors – the God of Abraham, the God of Isaac, and the God of Jacob – has sent me to you. This is my eternal name, my name to remember for all generations. (Exodus 3:14-15).

Yahweh Roh-i: is the Hebrew name meaning, the Lord is my Shepherd. As my Shepherd

I will trust You to guide and lead me along the pastures of life – through the rugged and smooth terrains that lie ahead. I understand that you have sent your Son to lead us closer to You, to shepherd us, and in this I shall lack no good thing.

Scriptures:

Hebrews 9:15 NIV

"For this reason Christ is the mediator of a new covenant, that those who are called may receive the promised eternal inheritance, now that he has died as a ransom to set them free from the sins committed under the first covenant."

Galatians 3:28 AMP

"There is [now no distinction in regard to salvation] neither Jew or Greek, there is neither slave nor free, there is no male or female, for you [who believe] are all one in Christ Jesus [no one can claim spiritual superiority]."

1 Peter 2:9 ESV

"But you are a chosen race, a royal priesthood, a holy nation, a people for his own possession, that you may proclaim the excellencies of him who called you out of darkness into his marvelous light."

Ephesians 2:10 NKJV

"For we are his workmanship, created in Christ Jesus for good works, which God prepared beforehand, that we should walk in them."

1 Timothy 2:3 KJV

"For this is good and acceptable in the sight of God our Saviour; who will have all men be saved, and to come unto the knowledge of truth."

These scriptures testify to who we are in Christ.

Reflect on your spiritual journey.

"And the testimony is this, that God has given us eternal life, and this life is in his son."
(1 John 5:11 NKJV)

Chapter VII
Testimony

While at work, I met an inquisitive, strong-willed woman whom I was honored to mentor. Her intrigue regarding my non-Christian but "spiritual path" was uncomfortable. I sensed her concern for me. She introduced me to a prayer line, which consisted of a group of women that would meet at 5:30 every morning to pray and read scriptures. They would also meet for charitable events in the community. I was urged to join, despite cringing at the idea of meeting so early in the morning and praying with a woman I did not know. But prayer was something that was not unfamiliar. I eventually joined the calls anonymously, not saying a word and remaining on mute. I would hear the name of Jesus being recited over and over and over. Hearing the name of Jesus was jolting. I was extremely uncomfortable hearing and saying Jesus' name. When it became too much I would leave the call and return to my bed of tears. The group was dynamic and full of life. Each woman had a story, a trial, a testimony, as well as victories. There was comfort in praying with the group however, so I continued to listen in and tried to tune out the name. Soon it became a morning routine and I was introduced to the "Daniel Fast" after a few months.

The Daniel fast is a 21-day fast that is based on the fasting done by the prophet Daniel in the Bible. It consisted of a strict vegan diet that prohibits certain foods and drinks. I had no reservations about this fast at all. We fasted and continued to pray and study the scriptures together. I said to myself, "I've got this. If I could get through 24 hours of complete fasting (Yom Kippur) for years, I should be fine. What's 21 days of fasting on healthy food?" I was in for a surprise. This was a fast like no other for me. By 14-21 days I became weary spiritually and physically. I felt naked and stripped bare. It was very hard to make sense of my emotions, and hunger was getting the best of me. I was no longer able to turn to my comfort foods nor was I able to overindulge. Because I still lived with my parents at that time, my dad did most of the cooking. He prepared meals that were not in line with the fast, and because I was working during the days I wasn't able to eat much of what was allowed during the fast. One particular morning I cried out to the Lord. I fell on my knees, cried, and prayed, asking God to reveal the Truth to me. What was missing from a young age? My heart was bent on knowing who He was. I desired to know the Truth and asked, "Is it Jesus? Is Jesus the missing piece? Because if He is, I don't know Him. I know what these people say and what's probably written about Him but I don't know Him. Help me to get to know Him." I pleaded in prayer for God to reveal Him to me and then left for work.

The first patient of the day was Michael. Michael was a diabetic who scheduled with me for intensive case management. Each patient visit was accompanied by a health educator and a clinician. Michael, along with the health educator, and myself were in the examination room. After an introduction Michael began to share his story. He shared his struggle with diabetes, his near death experience, and that he was married and lived in Florida. But then he cut the story short and proceeded to tell me that he was not in the clinic to speak about his story. He proceeded to say he came to the clinic to tell me that Jesus was waiting for me. "I came here to tell you that Jesus is waiting for you," he said. "And just as Moses went into Egypt and brought the children of Israel out of slavery and out of bondage, so Jesus is also waiting to bring you out of bondage," he asserted. There was a part of my spirit that instantly connected to his words. My mind struggled to make sense of it. How did this man know what words would captivate me? I had been immersed in the Old Testament for years. I had the story of Moses ingrained in my mind from the years of being an Israelite. *I was able to visualize an outstretched arm drawing me out and saving me from a life of sin and darkness* – Moses lifting his staff over the water as instructed by God to free the Israelites. I cried.

As the tears flowed, my mind was confused but my heart was soothed. As I looked over at the health educator, she also began to cry and was very much in tune to what was happening. I do remember him asking me about my husband. He asked for his name and told me to pray for him. He mentioned that demons had taken him over and said to continue to pray for him. I didn't understand what that meant at the time. Did he say demons? I saw Michael once after that encounter, maybe a week or two later. Despite my reluctance to accept Jesus, I did have a strong desire for Truth and a persistent desire and longing to know and grow closer to God. Those words spoken by the patient that day spoke to my spirit and soul. A sense of relief and gratitude gripped me

God delivers. He delivered the children of Egypt out of the slavery and bondage by the hand of Moses, and He delivered me! He can also deliver you! The mental, spiritual, and emotional bondage I was in was taking a toll on me. I felt controlled by it and made horrible decisions because of it. This bondage is comparable to that of the Israelites' bondage in the land of Egypt. The Israelites were physically in chains in Egypt. The bondage is the same, but guess what, we are now free in Christ. Moses led the way through dry land with a promise of salvation.

Jesus makes a way for us in the midst of our storms. He will make a way for you to rest and be still. Jesus says, "Come to me all who labor and are heavy laden, and I will give you rest."(Matthew 11:28 ESV). We can BE STILL and TRUST God to LEAD us. Take active steps toward Him. **No shrinking back.** Walk through on the dry lands that are before you as He parts the sea. He makes a way when there may appear to be no way. Do not fear, the waters have been parted for you. Don't fear the sin that crouches at your door. It has no hold on you if you remain obedient and trust in Elohim. We have freedom from fear, freedom from the condemnation of the law, and freedom from the realms of evil, sin, and corruption.

The Passover lamb's blood was also symbolic in the scripture. It was a means of deliverance for the Israelites, saving them from death. Moses directed all the elders of Israel: "Go and take for yourselves lambs according to your families, and slay the Passover *lamb*". Then the lamb's blood was applied to the doorposts of the Israelites homes (Exodus 12:7, 22). The blood was a sign of protection for the Isrealites from the angel of death. If the lamb's blood was not applied to the houses of the Israelites, their first-born, along with the Egyptian first-born, would be killed. Similarly, the apostle Peter, referring to the death of Jesus, wrote about being "sprinkled with His blood" (I Peter 1:2). He believed that Jesus, the Passover Lamb, was slain to save us from spiritual death. "Christ our Passover also has been sacrificed" (I Corinthians 5:7). In the Greek translation of the Jewish Scriptures, the second book of the Bible is called *Exodon*, meaning "the way out." Moses and Aaron said to Pharaoh, the King of Egypt, "Let My people go that they may celebrate a feast to Me in the wilderness." (Exodus 5:1).

The Lord made "a way out" for the Israelites, setting them free from slavery. Jesus spoke of "His departure, which He was about to accomplish at Jerusalem" (Luke 9:31). The word "departure" is a translation of the Greek word *exodon*. Jesus accomplished a spiritual exodus, setting human beings free from spiritual death. The Passover lamb had to be without any defects, in perfect condition. As the Lord said, "Your lamb shall be an unblemished male" (Exodus 12:5). Only the best could be offered, because it was a "Passover sacrifice to the Lord" (Exodus 12:27). We rejoice and revel in the fact that we are redeemed and saved by the "precious blood, as of a lamb unblemished and spotless, in perfect condition and without sin – *the blood* of Christ" (I Peter 1:19).

Reflection:

Let us reflect on one of the names of God:

The **ELOHIM** is the Hebrew title of God. It means supreme power. It is by this supreme power that the heavens and Earth were created. The use of the name in Genesis denotes an all-powerful, omnipotent, omnipresent, and creative Power. This very Power is able to create the universe, light out of darkness, and bring life into existence. It is known to be plural, which may hint at the vastness of His power. This divine power lives inside every believer. The same power that raised Jesus from the dead lies in us. The scriptures tell us that God, represented by a pillar of fire and smoke, led the children of Israel out of Egypt. Moses brought the Israelites out of bondage/Egypt and Jesus has brought us out of the bondage of sin and death. God was with Moses, the Israelites, and Jesus, and He is with us. We can look to Him for guidance and protection through life. With *great power* we are led to salvation. Israelites passed through the waters as Moses stretched out his hand over the sea in obedience and faith as commanded by God. His action paved the way for God's people. Jesus obedient to death has saved us from a life of sin. Praises be to our God, Elohim.

El Roi: the Hebrew name for God meaning the God who sees me. The God who sees me also sees you. His eternal love for us is evident in the mystery of His Son . His divine plan is to save creation from itself. The Son, Jesus-Yeshua, can be translated to "God saves or the salvation of God". He is the radiance of God's glory and the exact representation of His being, *sustaining all things by His powerful word.* After he had provided purification for sins, he sat down at the right hand of the Majesty in heaven" (Hebrews 1:3).

Scriptures:

Psalm 34.4 NIV

"I sought the Lord, and He answered me; He delivered me from all my fears"

Exodus 14:15-21 KJV

"And the Lord said unto Moses, Wherefore criest thou unto me? speak unto the children of Israel, that they go forward: But lift thou up thy rod, and stretch out thine hand over the sea, and divide it: and the children of Israel shall go on dry ground through the midst of the sea. And I, behold, I will harden the hearts of the Egyptians, and they shall follow them: and I will get me honor upon Pharaoh, and upon all his host, upon his chariots, and upon his horsemen. And the Egyptians shall know that I am the Lord, when I have gotten my honour upon Pharaoh, upon his chariots, and upon his horsemen. And the angel of God, which went before the camp of Israel, removed and went behind them; and the pillar of the cloud went from before their face, and stood behind them: And it came between the camp of the Egyptians and the camp of Israel; and it was a cloud and darkness to them, but it gave light by night to these: so that the one came not near the other all the night. And Moses stretched out his hand over the sea; and the Lord caused the sea to go back by a strong east wind all that night, and made the sea dry land, and the waters were divided."

John 15:26-27 AMP

"But when the [a] Helper (Comforter, Advocate, Intercessor – Counselor, Strengthener, Standby) comes, whom I will send to you from the Father, that is the Spirit of Truth who comes from the

Father, He will testify and bear witness about Me. But you will testify also and be my witness , because you have been with Me from the beginning."

Hebrews 11:29 KJV

"By faith they passed through the Red sea as by dry land: which the Egyptians assaying to do were drowned."

Hebrews 2:14-15 KJV

"Forasmuch then as the children are partakers of flesh and blood, he also himself likewise took part of the same; that through death he might destroy him that had the power of death, that is, the devil; And deliver them who through fear of death were all their lifetime subject to bondage."

Nehemiah 9:11 KJV

"And thou didst divide the sea before them, so that they went through the midst of the sea on the dry land; and their persecutors thou threwest into the deeps, as a stone into the mighty waters."

Psalm 77:16-20 AMP

"The waters [of the Red Sea] saw You, O God;

The waters saw You, they were in anguish; The deeps also trembled.

The clouds poured down water; The skies sent out a sound [of rumbling thunder];

Your arrows (lightning) flashed here and there. The voice of Your thunder was in the [a]whirlwind; The lightning illumined the world; The earth trembled and shook.

Your way [of escape for Your people] was through the sea, And Your paths through the great waters, And Your footprints were not traceable. You led Your people like a flock by the hand of Moses and Aaron [to the promised goal]."

1 Peter 2:24 AMP

"He personally carried our sins in His body on the [a]cross [willingly offering Himself on it, as on an altar of sacrifice], so that we might die to sin [becoming immune from the penalty and power of sin] and live for righteousness; for by His wounds you [who believe] have been [b]healed."

Romans 6:22 NIV

"But now that you have been set free from sin and have become slaves of God, the benefit you reap leads to holiness, and the result is eternal life."

These scriptures testify of Christ as a strong Deliverer.

"For as the body without the spirit is dead,
so faith without works is dead also."
(James 2:26 NKJV)

Chapter VIII
What Have You Done?

After the profound spiritual encounter that altered the trajectory of my life, I found myself standing at a crossroads, unsure of how to navigate the uncharted territory that lay ahead. The question lingered: What do I do now, after something like that happened to me? A few weeks after my encounter with Michael, he returned to ask me what I had done. I was not quite sure how to respond to that question. What was I supposed to do? He informed me that he would be moving back to Florida and thanked me for medical help. Fueled by a newfound eagerness to delve into the teachings of Jesus, I embarked on a fervent quest – praying more and immersing myself in the Old and New Testament with an insatiable hunger for knowledge.

As my eagerness intensified, so did my anxiety. The fear of playing catch-up and the pressure of becoming a Christian weighed heavily on my shoulders, leading to shame and self-righteousness. It was a tumultuous internal struggle that threatened to overshadow the spiritual growth I was experiencing. In the midst of this turmoil, I found some solace in a humble bathtub, baptized by a childhood friend, with members of the prayer line and my children as witnesses. She and her husband are pastors and had tried her hardest for years to minister to my ex-husband and I. As she immersed my body in the water, the song "For Your Glory" echoed in my heart – a song that became an anthem of surrender and devotion for me. "For your glory, I will do anything, just to see You and behold You as my King". I was acknowledging my acceptance of Jesus Christ as my Lord and Savior publicly. I accepted Him in my heart after meeting the patient, Michael. Thanks be to God for His grace and mercy.

The question of finding a church home now loomed over my head. With uncertainty overshadowing me, I initially returned to a Catholic church with my children in search of familiarity. I was led to a warm and inviting congregation – a home church where the authenticity and closeness of the community was like a balm for my soul. It was a place where I could be real and a place that felt tangible and genuine. My children and I grew spiritually in the intimate space of this congregation. From the fellowship in the backyard under a tent, to the small gatherings in the living room with song, dance, piano and guitar players in front of a wood burning fireplace, our gatherings were extraordinary. I had experienced nothing like it before. My mind and soul were nourished.

One pivotal moment occurred during a woman's retreat in June of 2018. That moment was etched into the pages of my journal. The pastor prayed, ministered, and prophesied over each individual. When Pastor J turned to me, her words resonated with divine truth: "Stop shrinking back. Stand in your glory. The spirit of tiredness leaves in the name of Jesus. Do you know who you are? No more backing down. No more shying away. No more tears. Walk in confidence. There is work to be done! Go! Pursue glory. Run!" In that sacred space surrounded by supportive women, a breakthrough occurred. The weight of unworthiness was lifted and was replaced by a newfound confidence. The women cheered, and I ran – both physically and metaphorically. As I ran through the retreat grounds, tears mingled with prayers, releasing the burdens I had carried for too long. Seated by a peaceful pond, I continued to pray, acknowledging the transformation taking place within me. The memory of that spirit-filled run and the pastor's powerful words became a cornerstone of my spiritual journey. **No more tears! No more shying away from whom God has created me to be.**

With gratitude, I ran back into the room, embracing my new posture with a heart overflowing with thanks. The journey of spiritual awakening had not only uncovered my identity but had also empowered me to stand boldly, free from the shackles of shame and self-righteousness. The pursuit of understanding my true self, and the encouragement of a loving community became a pillar upon which I continued to build. My evolving spiritual path commanded action. Faith with works! Faith in action! **No shrinking back!** I will walk through on dry land, glorifying and honoring God. Loving and teaching as commanded.

I have since acclimated to a home-based biblical research, teaching, and fellowship group that is dedicated to delivering the accuracy and practicality of God's Word. I challenge myself to avoid shrinking back and actively pursue consistent fellowship and outreach. I desire to have a home-based fellowship of my own to share intimate spaces with others who desire to grow closer to God and learn His divine Truths. The character of God is revealed to us through the Word. The names mentioned earlier in the book highlight the nature of our Creator. "As I study and learn more of You Father, I pray to glorify You all the more." "Creation in much of its beauty and splendor also reveals the glory of God" (Psalms 19:4). "The heavens proclaim the glory of God. The skies display his craftsmanship. Day after day they make Him known. Within the heart of every person, God has planted a desire to know Him (Ecclesiastes 3:11). As we seek we shall find. When we find HIM we are to display the aspects of who He is, in action and deed.

"For Your glory, I will proclaim Your magnificent works. I will continue to use my testimony to magnify Your name. My logical defense is prepared to give account for my hope and confident assurance in YOU."

Reflection:

Let us reflect on one of the names of God:

Emmanuel means, "God with us." He is with us in every situation. He will never abandon us or leave us. Seek Him as He seeks you. "Do you want to be well?" Jesus asked the invalid at the pool. "Do you believe that I am able to do this?" asked Jesus. He is ever-present to draw us closer to Him. We must have faith and seek Him with our whole heart, soul, and mind. What will you do when he saves you? What will you do when he heals you? Do what is to be done.

Scriptures:
Romans 10:8-10 NKJV

"But what does it say? "The word is near you, in your mouth and in your heart" (that is, the word of faith which we preach): that if you confess with your mouth the Lord Jesus and believe in your heart that God has raised Him from the dead, you will be saved. For with the heart one believes unto righteousness, and with the mouth confession is made unto salvation."

John 5:6-8 NIV

"When Jesus saw him lying there and learned that he had been in this condition for a long time, he asked him, "Do you want to get well?" "Sir," the invalid replied, "I have no one to help me into the pool when the water is stirred. While I am trying to get in, someone else goes down ahead of me." Then Jesus said to him, "Get up! Pick up your mat and walk."

Matthew 9:27-30 NIV.

"As Jesus went on from there, two blind men followed him, calling out, "Have mercy on us, Son of David!" When he had gone indoors, the blind men came to him, and he asked them, "Do you believe that I am able to do this?"

"Yes, Lord," they replied. Then he touched their eyes and said, "According to your faith let it be done to you"; and their sight was restored. Jesus warned them sternly, "See that no one knows about this."

1 Peter 3:15-16 AMP

"But in your hearts set Christ apart [as holy – acknowledging Him, giving Him first place in your lives] as Lord. Always be ready to give a [logical] defense to anyone who asks you to account for the hope and confident assurance [elicited by faith] that is within you, yet [do it] with gentleness and respect. And see to it that your conscience is entirely clear, so that every time you are slandered or falsely accused, those who attack or disparage your good behavior in Christ will be shamed [by their own words]."

James 2:14, 18 NKJV

14 "What does it profit, my brethren, if someone says he has faith but does not have works? Can faith save him?[18] But someone will say, "You have faith, and I have works." Show me your faith without your works, and I will show you my faith by my works."

These scriptures testify of Christ to be Savior and Lord.

"Therefore we do not become discouraged [spiritless, disappointed, or afraid]. Though our outer self is [progressively] wasting away, yet our inner self is being [progressively] renewed day by day. For our momentary, light distress [this passing trouble] is producing for us an eternal weight of glory [a fullness] beyond all measure [surpassing all comparisons, a transcendent splendor and an endless blessedness]"! (2 Corinthians 4:16-17 AMP)

Chapter IX

Processing Pain

In the face of pain I struggled to pray. Did I know how to? Did I want to? Would it help? The pain in the truth of the, *I told you so* was jolting. It pierced like a knife, especially when it came from my mother. Shortly after I found out that I was pregnant, mom and dad met my ex-husband and his mother and were able to deduce quickly that this match would not last. My mother angrily told me that I should leave him alone, and she mourned when I decided otherwise. My parents mourned. It was so hard for them not only to process my pregnancy but also to process my permanent connection to a man and a family they knew nothing about. I was in my last year of nursing school and didn't have a job or money to support a family. My extended family is large, loving, and supportive. My maternal and paternal family are native to Jamaica, and they worked to pave the way for their families. Members of my family are proud and respectable members of their hometown and their respective cities. It hurt me to know that they may have been embarrassed and ashamed of me in those moments.

The pain of knowing that my husband had succumbed to all that he struggled with as a child was unnerving. His disdain for his absentee biological father would repeat in the lives of our children.

He disregarded his father for abandoning him during his youth and has now followed in his father's footsteps. While I have no regrets, I wish I had made better choices and stood firm on the principles that I knew to be true. I am learning to love and respect myself now, in spite of my poor decisions. I tolerated too much due to my own lack of self respect and self confidence. However, I do believe that the Lord makes all things work for the good of those who love Him. While there are more stories of betrayal and heartache, I will refrain from sharing so as to remain respectful of the privacy of others.

The pain of seeing my father and brother mourn over the severed relationship was uncomfortable. After having objections to our union initially, my family had grown to love him. Seeing my father cry after having to ask my ex-husband to leave our home due to worsening addiction and behavior, kept replaying in my head. I have seen my father cry only a handful of times. My nephew heard my ex-husband's pleas nights after he was asked to leave. He would knock at the basement window for help. My ex-husband's father and step mom tried to offer solace. They tried to assure me by stating, "You're better without him. He never loved you." As I mourned, so did my mom – I believe she is still heartbroken for me and her grandchildren. Everyone was so confused. They would make comments such as, "Everything seemed fine," "He was such a great father," "How did this happen?" My emotional pain soon manifested into chronic chest pain and insomnia. The addition of work-related stress added to the strain on my body, yet my emergency room and medical visits yielded negative findings. My body was processing the emotional pain.

The pain of raising four children without a father was the very thing I feared. I tried to numb the pain with work, school, shopping, social media, and dating. The fear of not meeting their needs gripped me. At the height of my ex-husband's addiction, I had a young baby and three children. There were multiple calls from the hospital because he was found intoxicated. The emotional, financial, and physical duress was taxing and oftentimes caused me to fall into despair and self-pity. The embarrassment of him lying sprawled out on the lawn for neighbors to see was heart wrenching. Those painful moments have left scars. Those embarrassing scenes played out for at least a year before I finally decided to pack everything up and move back in with my parents. The more I prayed for truth and guidance, the more revelation came. My ex-husband's behavior pushed me to the edge. The drinking intensified, along with late night conversations with the potential second wife – a butt call would later reveal more infidelity as well as romantic encounters with the nanny and the frequent hospitalizations. I was done! **NO shrinking back**. No more ignoring the obvious.

They tried to warn me, but I thought love would fix it. I thought love was the answer to a man's broken heart. I believed our faith, coupled with our love, were enough. I shrunk in the face of an overwhelming reality: I cannot change another person's behavior. My ex-husband has his demons and he alone is to face them. I knew we were not equally yoked. Our backgrounds and values were different. Our love for one another was undeniable but love was not enough. The desires of our hearts coupled with action and intention are vital. Shrinking back can seem easy when processing pain. Hiding in a dark corner to avoid the inevitable seemed easier than confronting it. Avoiding friends and gatherings, procrastination, overspending, and overworking, were all unhealthy ways I was processing my pain. I shrunk and kept shrinking and then I prayed. I prayed fervently to the Lord and he heard my cry.

The move took one day. I told no one of my plans other than my parents. My ex-husband had just returned home from the ED after being found intoxicated on the street. The children were ages one, four, six, and nine at the time – I had to leave. We had lived more than 60 miles away from family and friends and it became increasingly difficult to bear the burdens alone. I was already behind on my mortgage and my parents were eager for me to escape the prison that I was in with the children. The morning of the move, my best friend called me because she intuitively knew something was wrong. I hesitated in telling her, but she was persistent. She hauled ass and drove over 60 miles to assist me as I left my home behind. The children were taken out of school and whisked away to our family truck and the U-Haul truck behind it. There was numbness and defeat but also relief as we drove from Connecticut back to my childhood home. Embarrassment, pain, confusion, and anger would soon replace the numbness. My children would later speak of those unforgettable moments in their lives – my oldest two children, now adults, still have very vivid and painful memories of that day.

Bitterness continued to fester overtime. As I grew stronger in the Word I became more aware of the need to rid myself of bitterness and anger. I would like to say that it has been resolved, but that would be dishonest. I am praying for absolution. It rears its head during birthdays, school meetings, open houses, and graduations – the important events that concern the children. Processing and also embracing our reality remain a daily mountain that I have to climb. We are making lots of great memories together and I cherish each moment, good and bad.

As the children become adults and have difficulties coping with the complexities of life, I pray and hope that they will find ways to cope with their pain. I hope that they will lean on their faith, the Word of God, family, and community to avoid shrinking back, and I pray that they will rise in the face of storms. Al-Anon and family counseling, as well as consistent fellowship with believers, will also be beneficial as we continue to process the pain. As a primary care practitioner, I am honored to partner with patients to promote healing, and help to prevent and treat illnesses. Helping others on their healing journey continues to empower me. It is medicinal and I enjoy empowering others to be healthy and well. I am better able to empathize and provide compassionate human care due to my lived experiences.

Processing pain whether physical, mental, or emotional requires awareness and acceptance. It requires love and compassion for self and others. Reliance on our God of hope is also necessary. Hope allows us to endure patiently. God will wipe our tears and remove that which pains us. His restoration and redemptive love is our bandaid. His love is the salve for our wounds. We must endure and be reminded of the hope in the life to come. Hope does not disappoint! Pain can have a purpose. Our Creator can make all things work for our good, for the good of those who love Christ. "For I know the plans I have for you, declares the Lord. Plans for welfare and not for evil, to give you a future and a hope" (Jer 29:11). His word also says, "The Lord is close to the broken hearted and saves those crushed in spirit" (Ps 34:18). He heals and binds up wounds and provides strength for the flesh and heart.

Self-help strategies such as journaling, exercising, prayer, fellowship, grounding, music, deep breathing exercises, diet, nutrition, and professional interventions may help us along our healing journey. Ultimately we must lean on the living Word of God and trust God to see us through the storms of life, knowing that He is forever by our sides, and our salvation can only be found in Him. Storms are temporary. His word is eternal. Staff your life with individuals who will encourage and support you along your journey: health professionals that can promote health and wellness as well as disease prevention. Seek out professionals such as primary care clinicians and mental health providers.

The beautiful pearl that is treasured by many is formed from an irritant. Nacre is secreted around an irritant that has entered an oyster shell. It serves as a protective covering to shield the mollusk from parasites or foreign objects. The layers of nacre create the iridescent gem, the pearl. Physical wounds go through a series of stages: inflammation, where there is increased blood flow to allow for oxygen and nutrients to be transported to the wound; rebuilding, where red blood cells create new tissues and collagen and strengthening, where stronger tissue develops around the wound – our healed wounds can produce a precious pearl.

Reflection:

Let us reflect on one of the names of God:

Yahweh Shalom is the Hebrew name for God meaning, the Lord is peace. Let all those who seek thee rejoice and be glad in thee: let such as love thy salvation say continually THE LORD BE MAGNIFIED" (Psalm 40:16). May You be magnified through trials and tribulations as our hope is renewed continuously. May we seek You, Lord and find peace in every situation. **Miqweh Yisrael** is the Hebrew name for God meaning Hope of Israel. The God of hope will fill us with peace and joy. **Yahweh Rapha** is the Hebrew name for God meaning the Lord who heals. God is our Healer who heals mind, body, and soul. He is our Master Physician.

Scriptures:

Isaiah 43:2 KJV

"When thou passest through the waters, I will be with thee; and through the rivers, they shall not overflow thee: when thou walkest through the fire, thou shalt not be burned; neither shall the flame kindle upon thee."

Psalm 40:2-3 KJV

"He brought me up also out of an horrible pit, out of the miry clay and set my foot upon a rock, and established my goings. And he hath put a new song in my mouth, even praise unto our God"

Romans 5:3-5 NIV

"And not only this, but in our tribulations, knowing that tribulation brings about perseverance; perseverance proven character; and proven character, hope; and hope does not disappoint, because the love of God has been poured out within our hearts through the Holy Spirits, who was given to us."

Romans 15:13 AMP

"May the God of hope fill you with all joy and peace in believing [through the experience of your faith] that by the power of the Holy Spirit you will abound in hope *and* overflow with confidence in His promises."

Jeremiah 17:7-8 KJV

"Blessed is the man that trusteth in the Lord, and whose hope the Lord is.

For he shall be as a tree planted by the waters, and that spreadeth out her roots by the river, and shall not see when heat cometh, but her leaf shall be green; and shall not be careful in the year of drought, neither shall cease from yielding fruit."

Psalm 71:5 NLT

"O Lord, you alone are my hope. I've trusted you, O Lord, from childhood. Yes You have been with me from birth; from my mother's womb you have cared for me. No wonder I am always praising you."

Psalm 23:4 King James Version

"Yea, though I walk through the valley of the shadow of death, I will fear no evil: for thou art with me; thy rod and thy staff they comfort me."

Psalm 119:50 NASB

"This is my comfort in affliction, that Your word has revived me.

These scriptures testify of the Lord as a Comforter and Helper.

"But seek first his kingdom and his righteousness, and all these things will be given to you as well." (Mathew 6:33)

Chapter X
Waiting in Vain for Love

I caved into the idea of dating apps to find my man after encouragement from a coworker and friends. I had been separated and divorced for years and I thought it was time to move on. "There is no reason you should be alone," they would say. "It worked for so and so," they would further contend. My dating app experience was uncomfortable. I felt as though I was selling myself at the highest bid – as if I was placing an ad in a newspaper: single mom of four looking for love. I reluctantly joined hoping to find love. It didn't take long to connect with someone.

After filtering through a few contenders, I sent a message to an interest. He soon replied and we exchanged numbers and after our initial phone call on an unforgettable September evening, there was an immediate and surreal connection. Oh, was I riddled with anxiety. He was a single father, recently divorced. He was from the Caribbean – tall, athletic, and a teacher. I have always admired male teachers. He is a musician, songwriter, author, and very intelligent. Our conversations were like no other I've had with any other man. We had similar goals and experiences. We would speak for hours at a time. I told my family and friends about this man, who I believed was an answer to prayers after my past failed attempts at finding love. He checked all the boxes, or so I thought. My dream wedding that I was plotting on my virtual vision board was about to happen sooner than I expected. I became increasingly anxious when things seemed to not progress as I thought it should. I longed to actually meet him in person, which seemed to drag on for over a month or so. I grew very impatient and my insecurities and anxieties began to rear its head. I needed more time to heal. There were triggers that would surface with this friend that I now know was a necessary part of my learning to "love and heal myself". My attachment issues became obvious and I looked for validation from him in unhealthy ways.

What was my vision of love? My vision of love was idealistic. I believed that love, the feeling, was enough. If two individuals commit to loving each other nothing can oppose the union. After a few months it became clear that I was on a romantic rollercoaster ride all by myself. I had left my love interest on the line and boarded the roller coaster solo. My romantic joy ride included all the things I had always dreamed of except the other participant. His obligations to his children, parents, and ex-wife precluded him from boarding the ride.

In my mind, his busyness equated to lack of interest. Ghosting, poor communication and unmet expectations initially complicated things and continued to fuel my anxiety. I found myself at times begging or pleading with him to go out or to call. I was shrinking and settling for less, not having the courage to walk away. My insecurities became obvious. His initial interest and excitement eventually turned to concern regarding the foundation of the ride, thus leading to apprehension and avoidance. "You are amazing but if you don't know it, no one else will," said my love interest. That was no fault of his. He just wasn't interested. However, I stayed the course. That was a testament to the fact that I definitely needed more time to heal. "I thought you would be better," he said – this statement has ruminated in my mind for years. I did nothing, and said nothing in response to the comment. I shrunk. I allowed this man to tell me that I wasn't good enough. And instead of addressing it, I ignored it and continued to try to convince him that I was worthy. I tried desperately to convince him of my worth, while losing myself. "You're great but…" To ignore that and continue to engage was demeaning. I was shrinking back. In a desperate effort to be chosen, I agreed to be friends despite always wanting more. I lied to myself and him and continued to play small. Proving my worth became a project. I often took notes to remember things discussed in conversations to better understand recurring issues we had.

I did not feel safe. I would become very defensive and argumentative when triggered, causing more discontent between us. As the sole provider and the head of the household, I guess I reeked of masculinity. The soft and demure essence of a woman does not mix well with male energy. I became well acquainted with my triggers. Did I mention that my desire to be chosen had my nervous system in shambles? I tried so hard to prove my worth and to explain why my responses were reactive or why I had idealistic views on love. I romanticized love with whimsical and childlike thoughts or visions as if scripted from a romance novel.

Debates became a mainstay in our situationship. I make it hard to be chosen, and I am not able to be led, is what I was told. I seek to control an argument and question his role as a man and as a provider,

I was told. I was deemed too disrespectful to be chosen. What does this all mean? His rejection actually empowered me and has taught me the importance of introspection as well as grace. I have been able to examine my own thoughts, feelings, and generational issues concerning relationships. His rejection gave me the ability to look within and self reflect. Why wait around for someone to have such a long list of reasons not to choose me as a partner?

As I self reflected, I became more aware of repeated generational patterns. My beautiful mother is a bit of an aggressor in the family and maintains the "head of household" role. My grandmother and great grandmother for much of their lives were single and "independent black females". They both lived much of their lives single and were successful in everything they put their hands on. I am proud of the maternal strength, perseverance, beauty, and grace I have inherited.

The 'independent black woman' or the 'hard working black woman' is a title that I wish to have retired. I am tired of working so hard, alone. I am tired of being independent. Am I perpetuating generational patterns that are hindering or that deem me to be defiant and disrespectful? Is this my personality? Is this love? As I reflect on these things, the answer is, No. Love is not aggressive or controlling. It is not self-seeking. I recognized that I had anxious attachments. I craved love and yet may unconsciously push it away. My nervous system did not have the capacity to receive love. There remained a need to protect my heart from an unseen threat. The right one will never be "the right one" if I am always in a state of anxious attachment. I now understand that to receive healthy love, I must not fear or be in a state of defensiveness. Awareness is key.

I must not allow my unresolved trauma and my desire to be seen, heard, validated, and appreciated cause me to settle. **Stop shrinking back** from what you desire. God's love is built on the foundation of service and sacrifice. Romance is great but not at the heart of what is necessary for a successful relationship.

Learning to love myself has birthed from this experience. "The greatest commandment is to 'love the Lord your God with all your heart, all your soul, and all your mind,' and the second is to 'love your neighbor as yourself'" (Matthew 22:36-40). Self-love is important and is necessary in order to love another. Loving and seeking God is paramount. As I get on the "learning to love myself" train, I will not shy away from saying no to people and or situations that don't support my well being. It will be a nonstop ride to that which is promised to me. My childhood insecurities will not affect my future decisions anymore, especially my decision in choosing a partner. I will not settle or confirm.

Loving another extends to respecting and learning the needs and wants of the other. John 3:18 exemplifies the expression of love through actions and not merely in word or speech. It is when two individuals work incessantly to better themselves while meeting the needs of their chosen partner. It is unrealistic to meet every need of course, but the attempt to love as God loves us is a command. Love and respect are necessary components of a relationship, and both parties must remain dedicated to providing these to each other.

The ultimate responsibility of emotional fulfillment is our individual responsibility. Emotional fulfillment is possible only through Christ. Intimacy with God is essential. We are provided for in every way by God, our Provider – Yahweh *Yireh*, and our Husband,

Ish. I realized that after a few years, I would not be chosen. We were not able to meet the needs of one another and the crazy back and forth cycle needed to end. He is a great guy but not my guy. His kindness and respect for my children and family is much appreciated. I love and respect his family and children immensely and will cherish the memories always.

Despite becoming great friends, I had to end our relationship after six years – ending the relationship and beginning with lessons learned and patterns broken. No longer will I be told, "You are not enough." No longer will I acquiesce to the demands of someone who hasn't chosen me. No longer will I wait in line with you to get on the rollercoaster. No longer will I wait for you to love me the way I deserve. No longer will I wait in vain. My healing and self-discovery continues. My lover and husband awaits. As I write these words, I remain dedicated to serving the Lord with all my heart, mind, and soul, and in seeking the kingdom of God and His righteousness. With that as my priority, all these things shall be added unto me as it is made clear in scripture. I will wait for a love that is true. I deserve a love that is true.

"Daughter, spend your life loving. Not seeking love. Ocean
need not seek water."
(John, 2018)

Reflection:

Let us reflect on one of the names of God.

Yahweh-Yireh: the Hebrew name for God meaning the Lord will provide. God is our provider. He is our, **Ish,** the Hebrew name of God meaning husband. "When that day comes," says the Lord, "you will call me 'my husband' instead of 'my master.' I will make you my wife forever, showing you righteousness and justice, unfailing love and compassion. I will be faithful to you and make you mine, and you will finally know me as the Lord" (Hosea 2:16, 19-20). The love between a man and woman is a mirror image of God's covenant love for us. The relationship we have with God is to be as intimate as marriage can be. Marriages should reflect God's image. It entails loving and serving one another unconditionally and synchronizing our will with the will of the Father. God's love is purposeful. His love is filled with grace. We can wait and place our hope in God. In God alone will my soul wait.

Scriptures:

Genesis 2:18 KJV

"And the Lord God said, It is not good that the man should be alone; I will make him an help meet for him."

Psalm 62:5 KJK

"My soul, wait thou only upon God;for my expectation is from Him."

Song of Solomon 8:4,6-7

4 "I charge you, O daughters of Jerusalem, that ye stir not up, nor awake my love, until he please...6 Set me as a seal upon thine heart, as a seal upon thine arm: for love is strong as death; jealousy is cruel as the grave: the coals thereof are coals of fire, which hath a most vehement flame. 7 Many waters cannot quench love, neither can the floods drown it: if a man would give all the substance of his house for love, it would utterly be contemned."

Song of Solomon 3:4 KJV

"It was but a little that I passed from them, but I found him whom my soul loveth: I held him, and would not let him go, until I had brought him into my mother's house, and into the chamber of her that conceived me."

Ecclesiastes 4:12 KJV

"And if one prevail against him, two shall withstand him; and a threefold cord is not quickly broken."

These scriptures testify that God is the Place where true satisfaction is found.

"Everything changes the day you realize your pain is a seed for your power." Survive great pain and you learn to laugh at fear. You learn to live" (John, 2018)

"And if ye continue in my word, then are ye my disciples indeed; And ye shall know the truth and the truth shall make you free. …And if the son therefore shall make you free, ye shall be free indeed."(John 8:31-32 & 36)

Chapter XI
Grand Rising

Not shrinking back is a constant exercise. Not pulling away or ceasing to rise above circumstances is our life's work. Moving forward in faith with confidence is the goal. "Brothers and sisters, I do not consider myself yet to have taken hold of it. But one thing I do: forgetting what is behind and straining toward what is ahead, I press on toward the goal to win the prize for which God has called me heavenward in Christ Jesus" (Philippians 3:13-14). Never ceasing to declare His promises, all the while pursuing His will and Remain SALTY. God has called us to be the salt of the earth and the light of the world when we share the living hope with others; willfully choosing to believe what the Word of God says, no matter what is going on in life. In spite of my situation, I will trust my God. You will arise as you affirm His good will over your life. Keep going and don't stop! Cut fear down to size and faith will bloom. That is how we rise!

"Do you understand what I have done for you?" Jesus asked his disciples after washing their feet. Jesus in humility and servitude washed his disciples feet the night before he died as an example as to how we are to humbly serve and love one another. In rising we are to remember to also serve, and love others as Jesus did. There is no hierarchy or favoritism in the Kingdom of God. His love is for all. The colorful spectrum of humans he has created are all beloved images of God. As he loves so are we commanded to love. Would you wash your neighbor's feet? Can you consider the needs of another with grace and compassion?

Don't allow your own, or anyone else's low expectations to cause you to shrink back. At the core of my existence lies the fundamental question, "Who am I?" I am a child of God. All opposing forces or negativity I encounter in this world will serve as encouragement for me to persist on this journey of self-discovery and growth. I firmly assert that the limits others may perceive are not mine to embrace. I will take captive my own negative thinking and make it obedient to Christ. I refuse to allow anyone's low expectations to force me into shrinking back. Despite external doubts and despite attempts to diminish my confidence, I PERSIST. *I will refuse to shrink back*. Shrinking back is not an option for those who understand their purpose. It is surrender to the trials and tribulations, not allowing them to diminish the essence of who we are – purposed to be in Christ Jesus. It is not settling for less than has been promised . The Word details the will of God, and in aligning with that divine purpose, we find the courage to stand tall and unyielding.

I recognize the importance of acknowledging my light and finding productive ways to be seen in the world. I am committed to discovering more within myself, constantly pushing beyond perceived limitations and fear. It is a conscious choice to rise above my fear, insecurities, and past traumas. The power lies not in the expectations of others but in my unwavering commitment to define who I am and who I intend to become through Christ Jesus. Setting intentions becomes a powerful tool in shaping my journey, and I am mindful that true strength lies in persisting despite and in spite of all: setting my mind on Christ and the things that cannot fade away, transforming or renewing my mind with prayer, studying the Word, gratitude, and rest. I will embrace grace, confidence, and purpose as I stand tall. In the tapestry of life, woven with threads of humanity, there lies an inherent need for grace and compassion. It is a plea that resonates from every corner of existence: "I am human. Love me." In the quest for authenticity and self-discovery, the journey towards confidence and self-respect becomes a transformative odyssey. Grace and compassion will be the guiding stars.

Embrace your humanity, nurture confidence, and self-respect, and dare to chase the flames that ignite your soul. Transform the prisons of your own making into platforms of growth. Focus on the Word of God, express gratitude, and refuse to shrink back in the face of challenges. Evaluate your thoughts and set them on God and His Truth. For in doing so, you step into the fullness of who He has made you to be intricately woven into the divine tapestry of existence.

The call to "chase what sets your soul on fire" echoes through the corridors of ambition. It's a reminder that within each of us lies a passion waiting to be unleashed. To embrace this fervor is to dance with the essence of one's true self. Confidence becomes the driving force that propels us forward. To escape the self-made prisons that confine our potential, a fundamental shift in thinking is imperative. "To get out of the prisons I have made for myself, I will change my thinking." This declaration becomes a mantra, an anthem for breaking free from the constraints of self-doubt and negative perceptions. It is a constant exercise: day by day, hour by hour, and minute by minute.

Gratitude remains a foundational pillar on this journey. It is a humble acknowledgment of the blessings that surround us. Amidst the trials and tribulations, gratitude serves as a compass, guiding me back to the center of my purpose. Gratitude is a must. In counting our blessings, we find the strength to rise above challenges and setbacks. In the pursuit of a life marked by the abundance promised to us in scripture, a commitment to intentional give is a cornerstone. It is how I will rise above the confines of lack and insufficiency. I will cultivate abundance through purposeful giving. Recognizing the power of generosity, I embark on a journey of dedicating 5% of my income to a charitable organization and another 5% to a religious organization consistently. In dedicating a portion of my income to causes greater than myself, living within my means, working heartily unto the Lord, trusting in divine provision, and seeking financial guidance, I set the stage for a life of purposeful abundance and financial wisdom. No more negative balances. No more shrinking away from the abundant life that has been promised

The journey of ascending is a testament to the transformative power of intentional choices and an unwavering belief in the power of the All-Sufficient One: El Shaddai. True reliance on Him will yield a future marked by prosperity, purpose, and perpetual growth. The deliberate act of giving extends beyond mere financial transactions; it becomes a transformative force, reshaping my relationship with wealth and purpose. Living within means and breaking free from the poverty mindset is my goal. To truly embrace abundance, I commit to living within my means. This is not merely a financial strategy but a conscious choice to remove the poverty mindset that has lingered for far too long. It is an acknowledgment that my needs are distinct from my wants, and in this discernment, I find the freedom to break free from the shackles of scarcity thinking. This shift in perspective is a declaration that abundance is not solely about material wealth but encompasses a mindset that recognizes and appreciates sufficiency. I must continue to trust and have an unwavering belief that He has and will continue to provide for me. No more fear.

Embracing abundance is not about reaching a destination but about the continuous journey of ascending. The essence of the ascent lies not in the absence of challenges but in the resilience cultivated through them. In the quiet moments of reflection, I find myself marveling at the gifts bestowed upon me by the Creator – my four children. They are not just biological extensions but profound manifestations of divine grace; each one a unique masterpiece sculpted by the hands of my Creator. With a heart full of gratitude, I recognize that my role as a parent extends beyond providing the essentials. It is a sacred duty to pave the way for a future marked by faith. An awareness settles over me as I contemplate the generational pitfalls that have plagued my family in the past: insecurity, financial strain, mental illness, and addiction. I am resolute in my commitment that these patterns will not dictate the future for my children. Their destinies are not predetermined by the shadows of the past. Instead, I see before me a canvas of possibilities with Christ as the cornerstone.

I am aware that shrinking back is not an option. The abundant life promised is not just a distant dream; it is our birthright as children of God. In my unwavering faith, I find the strength to stand in the face of adversity and through the trials of life, setting a precedent for resilience and perseverance. In the eyes of my children, I see the reflection of my choices, my resilience, and my commitment to an abundant life. Each step forward is not just for me but also for them and the generations that will follow. In standing tall, I offer them a legacy of love, resilience, and the unwavering belief that they too can rise above any challenges that will come their way.

A profound shift occurs within me as I declare, "I am worthy and will not settle." No longer will I allow the echoes of my past insecurities to dictate my self-worth. The workaholic tendencies that served as a shield are no longer a refuge. Instead, I choose to engage with life, to savor its moments, and to be present for my children. It is a conscious decision to maintain healthy relationships with friends and family, recognizing that love and connection are essential elements of a fulfilled life. I am grateful for my family and friends. They have been a major source of stability and encouragement. Having come from small towns in Jamaica, they made great lives for themselves and their families. Hard work, ambition, grace, and strength are in my blood. I remain grateful for their presence in my life. I rise in acknowledgement of who I am in Christ and who I have descended from. My friends and mentors are blessings to me as well. They enrich my journey greatly.

There is no waiting in vain for love. I release anxious attachments. No longer will I strive to dominate in relationships. Instead, I embrace the beauty of balance, allowing my male counterpart to express love in ways that nature has designed. I will forever love my ex-husband and will remain in prayer for his health and salvation. I have forgiven him. Healing is a continuum and growth is inevitable. In doing so, I create an environment where love becomes the foundation upon which all things are built. Everything now builds on the love of God.

As Moses parted the waters to clear our path to salvation from the bondage of Egypt, Jesus in death has redeemed us from the curse of the law. His death on the cross frees us from the bondage of sin and death. We shall rise in Christ. The washing of the disciples' feet by Jesus is a demonstration of the humility and servitude offered to mankind. It can be viewed as a spiritual cleansing offered by Christ. The feet are the foundation of the human body. God's love is an internal wellspring that we can tap into and share freely. We are to show this same love and servitude demonstrated by Christ to others. Jesus came to serve. In rising we celebrate the value of salvation in Christ. The Spirit of God who raised Christ Jesus from death is alive in us! We rise with Christ! We have light in place of darkness. We have hope in place of despair. We have trust in place of fear. We have grace in place of shame. We choose freedom in place of domination. We have abundance in place of poverty. We can leave all the things that enslave us on the cross Jesus died on. We will walk in the light of His glory and walk along the dry ground to salvation as we choose. Paul's prayer in Ephesians is for our hearts to gain insight and to experience the hope of all God calls us to be. Let's rise to the calling.

Reflection:

Let us reflect on one of the names of God:

Yahweh Tsuri is the Hebrew name for God, meaning the Lord is my rock and **Yahweh Nissi**: the Hebrew name for God meaning, the Lord is my banner, mighty warrior, victory. Moses built an altar and named it Yahweh-Nissi to celebrate victory over the Amalekite. When Moses held the staff of the Lord high in his hands the Israelite army gained strength and defeated the mighty army. The battle is already won. The victory is ours by way of Jesus Christ. **We raise our banners high as we RISE!**

Scriptures:

Hebrews 10: 37-38

"In just a little while, he who is coming will come and will not delay. And my righteous one will live by faith. And I take no pleasure in the one who shrinks back."

Romans 8:11 NLT

"The Spirit of God who raised Jesus from the dead, lives in you. And just as God raised Christ Jesus from the dead, He will give life to your mortal bodies by this same Spirit living within you."

Ephesians 1:15 ESV

"For this reason, because of your faith in the Lord Jesus and your love toward all the saints, I do not cease to give thanks for you, remembering you in my prayers, that the God of our Lord Jesus Christ, the Father of glory, may give you the Spirit of wisdom and of revelation in the knowledge of him, having the eye of your heart enlightened, that you may know what is the hope to which he has called you, what are the riches of his glorious inheritance in the saints, and what is the immeasurable greatness of his power towards us who believe, according to the working of his great might that he worked in Christ when he raised him from the dead and seated him at his right hand in the heavenly places, far above all rule and authority and power and dominion, and above every name that is named, not only in this age but also in the one to come."

John 13:3-8

"Jesus knew that father had put all things under his power and that he had come from God and was returning to God; So he got up from the meal, took off his outer clothing, and wrapped a towel around his waist. After that, he poured water into a basin and began to wash his disciples' feet, drying them with the towel that was wrapped around him. He came to Simon Peter, who said to him, "Lord, are you going to wash my feet?" Jesus replied, "You do not realize now what I'm doing, but later you will understand. "No", said Peter, "you shall never wash my feet". Jesus answered, "Unless I wash you, you have no part with me."

These scriptures testify of Christ as Victor.

Prayer:

"Adoni,Lord and Master,

I come to Your throne with a renewed awe of Your greatness. I submit to You; I desire to learn Your ways so it may be well with my soul. I have found my words.

Praise be to Your holy name."

No turning back. I have decided to follow Jesus. I have decided to follow Him. The cross before me, the world behind me. NO TURNING BACK. No turning back. No turning back. No turning back. If I live, I'm living for You; and if I die, I'm dying for You . Whatever comes, let it be true. I'm following You.

Song by Steffany Gretzinger:
No Turning Back

Notes

(The Holy Bible, New International Version [NIV], 1973/2011)

(New King James Bible [NKJ], 1982/2004)

Amplified Bible. KJV. (2015). Bible Gateway. https://www.biblegateway.com (Original work published 1965).

Anekwe, O. (2014). Global Colorism: An Ethical Issue and Challenge in Bioethics. *Voices in Bioethics*, *1*. https://doi.org/10.7916/vib.v1i.6470

Fields, L. (2024). When Faith Disappoints: The Gap between what we experience and what we experience.

John, J. (2018). Daughter Drink This Water. Soul Water Rising.

Lynch, W. (1712). *Willie Lynch letters: The making of a slave.*

Quinn, C. (2019). Who has God chosen? And What About the Rest of Us? https://bibleproject.com/articles/who-has-god-chosen/

Wilkerson, I. (2020). Caste. Allen Lane

A Mother's Prayer for Her Children 2 (2020) Mother's Prayer retrieved from https://biblicalviewpoint.com/2020/07/31/a-mothers-prayer-for-her-children-2/#:~:text=A%20Mother's%20Prayer%20for%20Her%20Children%202,(Romans%2010%3A9).

www.ingramcontent.com/pod-product-compliance
Lightning Source LLC
Chambersburg PA
CBHW050442150626
46551CB00028B/1153